I dedicate this book to my mom—and to the angels that guide me on a daily basis.

1. Taylor Swift

Shanghai, China. The Mercedes-Benz Center.
May 2014.
Two days before my 20th birthday.

The drumming music started to shift as the crowd of people anxiously waited. The dark screen turned a menacing but vibrant red. A tall, slender shadow appeared behind the flowing transparency. Her voice echoed across the arena.

When I saw her, tears began rolling down my face.

It was Taylor Swift.

Girls were screaming hysterically, but I didn't hear them. A thousand emotions started to build up from the inside.

It's safe to say that Taylor Swift's music saved my life. That's not a cliché. Older people may not understand her the way I, and millions of others, understand her. The way she wrote about growing up and coping with human emotions inspired me, carried me, sustained me. Without her work, I wouldn't be a writer. Without her, I could not have survived.

The concert ended, but the battles with the illness in my brain have continued.

2. A large brain

At the time that I was born, Shanghai was still an unknown actress finding her way to stardom.

This was before the full economic growth of this bubbly city. Before the miraculous blossoming of the LuJiaZui district, with several of the tallest buildings in the world centered around the Huangpu River. Before CNN lavishly praised the city with an article hailing Shanghai as the best city in the world.

Back then, it was a place where Westerners tried to find their lost American dreams. It was a time when foreigners with blue eyes and blonde hair were still spectacles in the crowds. It was the place where my parents met and fell in love.

In Pudong.

Every family has its own book. The outlook of the book depends heavily on the storyteller. When the storyteller is happy, shadows are burned away with bright and beaming lights. For the first eight years of my life, our story was a happy one.

The first chapter of our family book is the arrival of a little girl with something special.

A large brain.

I'm not exaggerating. This isn't a metaphor, either. My head was so large that, even by age two, I couldn't hold my head upright. Forehead, occipital lobe, everything—all oversized. My family members insisted that my brain was an indication of intelligence. "*Qian tu hou tu,*" they would say, remarking on what a large brain I must have. As they expected, I was one of the smartest girls in my kindergarten, and later in primary school too, with excellent grades to back them up.

As an only child, I enjoyed love and attention from everyone. I had four grandparents who cared for and loved me deeply: my two grandmothers had huge arguments over who got to spend time with me. To this day, they still don't speak to each other when they meet at family dinners.

My dad is extremely tall by Asian standards. He's a prestigious surgeon in the best hospital in Shanghai. My mother is beautiful—her big bright eyes and her high cheekbones make her look like a movie star. Every week during the four years before their marriage, my father travelled all the way from Pudong to Puxi to see my mother. It was the longest and most painful trip anyone in Shanghai can take. He transferred buses four times, then took a boat, then walked a kilometer. After four years of his relentless effort, they were married.

And produced a baby girl.

Our family always ate together. My paternal grandparents lived with us, so my grandmother cooked for us . There were always fruits, cake, homemade soy milk, dumplings, and egg fried rice in the house. Ms. Chan also took on the role of entertainer. She is still the best storyteller I know, better even than my father. She had boundless energy and enthusiasm for everything in life.

3. ※

People are people, and sometimes it doesn't work out…

-"Breathe"

4. Stronger.

All hell broke loose when I was twelve. My grandfather passed away, and my grandmother left the house to live in her own apartment in Pudong district. Without her stability, my parents started arguing a bit.It's a cliché, but the story of how a happy child becomes depressed in a discordant environment is exactly how it played out. I felt my spirits sinking low.

Furthermore, my period also chose to arrive for the first time. Sometimes I couldn't even walk down the hall without feeling a spurt of blood roll down my legs.

There were other problems, too. The Chinese middle school exam was approaching, and I couldn't get my brain to concentrate. When I tried to study, a voice would appear inside my head and demand that I pay attention to the objects around me. My favorite pink pencil would start talking to me. *Ditch the geometry and look at me*, it would say.

To be clear, I wasn't schizophrenic. I wasn't hearing actual voices. These were merely thoughts that my brain was projecting onto the pink pencil. I ordered my brain to let go of the object.

I noticed that my left eye was more distractible than my right eye, so I started to do homework with my left eye squinted shut. It didn't help much. It felt as though there were a huge blockage in my brain that deterred me from using any of my memories and creative skills.

At school, I found that I couldn't talk any more. Even in the cafeteria, I couldn't utter a word. The conversations became one-sided, and I slowly became a bit alienated from everyone. There was one person who stood by me: my best friend Audrey. She was a shield between me and the rest of the classmates. She has this inner joy that lights up an entire room. She has wide large eyes that are extremely bubbly and bright. She earned straight As. And she was definitely the most popular girl in school. Under her influence and caring, my depression lifted and I started to come back to my true self. I also made a decision to only study at the library. The large empty house was not the same without my grandma's presence and with the ongoing battles between my parents.

The effect was nearly magical. The tranquil atmosphere in the Shanghai library healed me. As a matter of fact, my brain could concentrate for the entire day without interruption, finishing the most daunting tasks within minutes. I felt as though I had discovered a superhuman power. I started to further my learning in English and recited thousands of vocabulary words within a short period of time. Every second became magical.

When an opportunity to go to Harvard University for an eight-week-long secondary student program presented itself, I took the TOEFL test and got an almost perfect score. Harvard demanded an interview before fully accepting me into their summer program. The interviewer later described my English as "perfectly fluent and without any accent. She speaks like a girl who grew up in the U.S." A week later, Harvard formally accepted me. Although it was just summer school, at age fifteen, it meant the world to me. My early battles with my brain proved to have some values in building my strength. I became blindly optimistic that I would never again experience any form of depression or OCD or whatever those battles were. I had proven that I was stronger than the demons.

If only that had been true.

5. Harvard University.

On the flight from Shanghai to Boston, I read *Sophie's World* for six hours straight, absorbing myself in her beautiful and philosophical observations. *Wisest is she who knows she does not know.* Even better: *The only thing we require to be good philosophers is the faculty of wonder.*

I put the complimentary Häagen-Dazs in my mouth but barely tasted it. When the brain was happy, material things weren't necessary.

Eight weeks at Harvard University. It was designed to imitate the first year. I had access to every single facility that a normal Harvard undergraduate would have had. We lived on campus with very little amount of adult supervision. I started to learn all the inside jokes. I was told not to ever touch the John Harvard sculpture's feet because the graduating seniors pee on them for good luck.

A part of me was thrilled for the chance to be away from all the drama at home. Another part of me was frightened, but not by the typical things, such as culture shock or communication problems. After all, I already spoke English like a native.

Mine was deeper. I was afraid of losing control of my highly functioning brain. This created a hard lump of fear that sat in my chest like a stone. Whenever I thought about losing myself again, but this time in front of strangers, I pictured falling face-first onto the ground without pillows to catch me.

I was assigned to live in Lowell House. It had a large tower in the front, which made it look like a residency hall at an old English boarding school. Compared with other dormitories, it was located a little further from the main buildings and libraries. However, Lowell House boasted a little garden where students liked to socialize.

I quickly made friends in Lowell House. I shared a two-room suite with a lovely Asian-American girl named Renee, whose brother already was an undergraduate at Harvard and later on would be a graduate student at Johns Hopkins University. At an ice cream social on the first day, I met a girl from Colombia named Manuela. She told me that I was one of the most energetic girls she has ever met. It meant a lot, since she was one of those people whom others instantly like. The next morning, on my way to the dining hall, I met the most beautiful girl I had ever seen. She looked like angel from heaven. Her greenish large eyes, her long blonde hair, her legs—all these things, beautiful on their own, were accessories to a sparkling personality.

Even her name, Grace, reflected these things. Everything about her was in fact graceful, almost divine.

The four of us quickly became inseparable. Eating inside Annenberg Hall made us feel royal and magical. The Hogwarts' dining hall couldn't have felt more atmospheric than this place. Of course, such lofty architecture didn't stop us from hogging out on frozen yogurt together. Or making a hamburger with two beef patties, three slices of cheese, and an amazing amount of ketchup on top.

After the intense classroom work ended for the day, we would go on adventures in little cafes around the Cambridge area. On weekends we dressed up and went to age-appropriate and alcohol-free dance parties. I had never been to a dance party before, but I always went crazy the moment the music started playing. Any awkwardness in my limbs simply vanished. My girlfriends made me feel free. We held one others' hands as if we were sisters that had finally been reunited after fifteen years of separation.

We studied together, ate Doritos and chocolate cookies at midnight together, and laughed until our bellies hurt. They helped me set up my very first Facebook account. We uploaded countless crazy videos on YouTube. We even expanded our social circles by involving Lulu (an honest-to-God academic genius), Jonathan (a charmer who was secretly adored by Grace and was later accepted to U Penn along with my roommate Renee), Elly (a computer science whiz who went to Caltech after senior year) and Veronica (who was interning at a lab at MIT during this time and who later actually became a Harvard undergraduate). These people gave me validation that I needed—that I could get along with people from different cultures.

On one condition. I had to remain myself.

But I couldn't keep the depression away.

6. ※

You can take me down with just one single blow...

—"Mean"

7. Bipolar

The crash came towards the end of the second week. When my roommate Renee and I walked to the dining hall for breakfast, I could barely muster a word. I could sense her confusion. She didn't know how her roommate could vanish overnight.

I didn't know how that could happen, either. It didn't stop there.

As the weeks rolled by, my unsteady personality and behavior slowly caught the attention of most of the girls. One day, I locked myself in my room, refusing to leave. My friends had to drag me outside to experience the beauty of the campus. Other friends in Lowell House didn't notice, mesmerized as they were by the awesomeness and beauty of Grace, the queen of our little community. In fact, I felt the need to address my issues with somebody, so one day I told Grace that I seriously thought that I had bipolar disorder. It was a new term we had just learned in our law and psychology class, taught by Dr. Ellsworth Fersch, an interesting professor with silver hair who had published several books, including *Thinking About the Insanity Defense*.

Grace laughed. "Jiayi, I know you. You are definitely not bipolar."

End of discussion. I had self-diagnosed wrong, at least according to Grace. Then what was this invisible problem in my brain? I searched frantically through the DSM manual that the professor had recently given us.

Dissociative identity disorder (previously known as multiple personality disorder). Clinical depression. Attention-Deficit/Hyperactivity Disorder.

I read all the entries. Each had elements that seemed like my affliction. Could a person suffer from a combination of mental illnesses? I decided upon a solution. If I became a professional psychiatrist, I would be able to completely heal myself.

At the end of the eight weeks, when my mother's friends from New York came to pick me up, I was utterly distraught. Renee, Manuela, Grace—saying goodbye was wrenching. There were tears, hugs, more tears, more hugs. We promised to stay in touch forever. I stalled as long as I could before getting in the car, and cried as we pulled away.

On the airplane, I continued quietly sobbing. I was losing everything that stabilized me. The friends who loved me, the class schedule that gave meaning to every second of my day. The daily hibiscus tea at Peet's Coffee around the corner from the bookstore. Basking in the sunlight with my bare skin touching the grass in Harvard Yard. The nights battling the essays for Dr. Fersche's class in the computer lab that stayed opened 24 hours a day.

Those eight weeks had given me a sense of order and peace. I'd built a network of support, a routine that was dependable, predictable, and fulfilling.

Now it was ripped apart, leaving nothing to cushion my beautiful but unreliable brain.

The fifteen-hour plane ride felt like an eternity. This time, however, I couldn't read anything. My brain was consumed with one thought.

How to return to the U.S.

8. SSAT

Wearing a bright orange pair of flip-flops and jean shorts that couldn't have been any shorter, I jumped into my mom's arms at the airport in Shanghai.

On the ride home, I immediately started thinking about applying for boarding schools in the U.S. Part of it was caused my overwhelming grief upon leaving Harvard. Part was my fear of the start of high school in less than four weeks. A third part was feeling petrified of returning to the big lonely house, to the fights.

Ironically, returning to China proved to be the bigger culture shock. Wearing shorts and flip-flops outdoors became a habit, one that my conservative father protested. When meeting strangers on the streets in Shanghai, I couldn't make eye contact, even if anyone in this bustling city actually cared enough to try. In the evenings, I tried to use online proxies to break the Internet firewall to talk to my friends on Facebook. I looked at the thousands of photos that we had taken at Harvard, like a grieving mother who has just lost her beloved son.

It didn't take long before I began to search for a boarding school. In my research, I learned that I would have to prepare for the SSAT, which is a secondary school admission test. As a shorter version of SAT, the test contained vocabulary requirements that were almost equally difficult. I started throwing myself into the Shanghai library, reciting words and taking practice exams. In fact, preparing for the test was the only thing that calmed my brain down. It had a purpose that was congruent with my heart. The purple Kaplan SSAT vocabulary book accompanied me everywhere.

Then it started again.

You will never remember them, the notebook said. *Look at me. I will turn your brain into a bowl of noodles.*

No, said my blue ballpoint pen, *give your attention to me.*

I balled up my hair in my fists. I couldn't believe this was happening again. Before, the crazy talk only started in exams or stressful situations. Now it was playing out in the library, the one place that I had always been able to find peace and solitude. The one place that my brain was able to concentrate.

This is it. I stormed out of the Shanghai library and went home. I forced myself to sit in the European-style white chair in my bedroom. Then I starting writing personal essays for boarding schools in the U.S. Writing is pretty easy when you have a gun held to your head. For me, that gun was the thought of never going anywhere in life, of being forever stuck with my crazy brain. And the only apparent solution to avoid being stuck was to move back to the United States.

I threw myself into those applications. Three weeks later, I took the SSAT and scored an 85% on the test. I was genuinely happy. It meant I stood a chance of getting into most of the boarding schools in the U.S.

9. An interview

"Could you explain more about the psychology club?" asked Martin, my interviewer from Kent. He was looking at my school transcript, a little confused. Martin was my interviewer at Kent School, a beautiful boarding school in Connecticut.

"Psychology club is my favorite club at Shanghai Foreign Language School," I explained. "Everyone discusses questions and their issues openly in a nonjudgmental environment. Such as how to deal with peer pressure."

I wondered whether they would have something like this at Kent, because Martin seemed even more confused.

"You just can't help feeling joyful once you step into the counseling center in my school,n my sch. "Eric, the most beloved English teacher on campus, said that this room had saved his life many times. We all agreed that Ms. Zhu, the super sweet and beautiful counselor, was a blessing to all of us."

I thought back to what Eric had once said in that room, during an event held by the psychology club. He had wondered aloud why all his students hated him. "They are never interested in what I have to say.' Our counselor Ms. Zhu replied, " are you interested in what you have to say in class?" The question got Eric thinking. Later, he started to put a lot more enthusiasm into what he was doing and came back as possibly the most popular teacher ever in the history of Shanghai Foreign Language School.

"We do have a counselor on our campus. Martin's voice pulled me back from reminiscing about the past. "What role did you play while participating in the psychology club?"

I decided to ignore the fact that it stabilized my erratic moods. Instead, I detailed all the events I planned with the members and how the psychology club had won a regional award for school clubs in Shanghai.

Martin later wrote to me that he knew Kent and I would be a great match, as I was among the brightest and smartest candidates he had interviewed.

I wondered what he saw in me.

Before the beginning of high school, I received a letter from Martin.

I was accepted.

To Kent School.

I was speechless. One of the best boarding schools in the state wanted me. In other words, I could go back to the U.S. A place that contained magic, a place where my mental conditions might heal. Since the competition for international students was ridiculously fierce that particular year, I became convinced that a hidden force must have helped me.

Mental illness suddenly became something of the past. I regained my ability to focus, everything started to flow. My English started to improve itself even further. *Maybe I haven't failed in this world.* I wrote in my pink diary. *I'm still alright.*

For the moment.

10. 15

And when you're fifteen feeling like there's nothing to figure out but count to ten, take it in. This is life before you know who you're gonna be…

--"Fifteen"

11. Sweet Sixteen

I couldn't believe my ears. All fifty-two party guests, my friends and family, were singing my favorite song, the one about being young and not knowing what to do. And they were singing it *at me*. In English.

The problem was that I wasn't fifteen anymore.

I was now sixteen.

We were in the magnificent Grammy room in HAOLEDI, the largest room in the largest KTV chain in the city. The room had a mini-stage and six microphones for dancers and singers. My friends in Shanghai had been planning this birthday party for months. They even asked all my friends to recite those English words so that everybody could sing together.

My sweet sixteen.

I opened my presents. A pink diary. A Swavroski pendant. A best-selling novel. A designer notebook. A souvenir picture frame. One friend surprised me with a huge birthday book, containing everyone's words of encouragement. Their love was splashed on every single page. I couldn't believe that my Chinese friends had done this for me, that I was special enough for them to make this day special.

I looked up from the gifts and realized something. This wasn't just a sweet sixteen. This was also a farewell party. I was leaving for Kent School in a month. All this time, I had only been listening to my own screams of desire to run away. I'd forgotten that I meant something to them, too.

The party ended, of course, late in the evening, the singing and the laughter fading away.

A few weeks later, on a gloomy morning at Shanghai airport, my parents and grandparents faded away quietly too. I remember seeing them wave sadly at me as I entered customs.

I suddenly felt I had made a terrible mistake. *Will the old ghosts walk away forever? Will I keep being this strong? Will everything be all right?* Tears blurred my eyes, but I forced myself to stop thinking, to keep going.

I was starting on a journey to reinvent myself.

12. Middle South Girls' Dorm

It was dim when I first laid eyes on Kent in the distance. I was inside the Cadillac SUV that the school had sent to pick me up at JFK airport. Flashing past the window was a blurry scene of trees, rivers, and more trees.

The other students sitting in the car, two seniors, seemed nonchalant about the scene. The driver with silver hair kept chatting with us as we sailed through the forest. His bubbly personality was in stark contrast to my reticent character.

As we arrived on the campus, I saw that it was extraordinarily beautiful—wooden houses, colored brick buildings, natural scenery that resembled a Monet from every angle.

The driver stopped the car, stepped out, and set my luggage on the curb. I dragged it down a ramp covered with red and golden leaves to my assigned dorm room on the rear of the south building.

The students at Harvard had seemed to be easygoing and friendly. I didn't think it would be too hard for me to fit in here. I would just be myself, the way I'd been at Harvard.

As I dragged my two large suitcases up to the third floor, other questions ran through my mind. Would this school provide answers to my problems? Would I be able to survive for the next three years?

At last, I found my room. Number 305. On the door was a sheet with two names. *Maggie H.Jiayi H.*

Maggie and I had already Skyped several times. She seemed like a really outgoing girl. By stalking her Facebook profile, I knew that she was the kind of all-American girl who easily gets a hundred likes on her photos. And while I knew that Facebook likes didn't mean everything in the world, it still made me a little jealous.

The first week went surprisingly well. On the first day of school, Maggie publicly told her friends that she liked me very much as a roommate. She said she could tell that I was kind and smart. I also heard her tell her parents on the phone that I was the best roommate she had ever had. Maggie seemed to be a kind person.

I made my own friends, too, on the second floor of the middle south girls' dorm. Most of the girls were very pretty. There was a model from Argentina who had done runway shows in Milan. She had the thinnest physique I'd ever seen. There was also a girl who had been modeling since she was eight years old. She was six feet two inches tall. Her blonde hair and blue eyes sparkled as if God had sent her to show the degree of perfection his creation could achieve. Coming from a strict family in Shanghai and having no knowledge of styling or makeup tools, I felt like an ugly duckling next to them.

Despite the school's beauty, it was way too crowded in the dormitory. And as a sophomore, I wasn't allowed to apply for a single room yet. It was a struggle every time I went outside. There was nowhere to be alone. I memorized the class schedule of my roommate so that I could slip in some personal time alone in our room. The problem was her popularity. Even when Maggie was in class, her friends—and there were a lot—regularly knocked on the door and asked her whereabouts. One time, when I was in the room reading alone, two of her friends came in, unannounced, and took two large bags of Doritos from our shared fridge. I didn't even have time to protest that I'd bought them the day before.

I decided to lock the door whenever Maggie was in class.

On a Monday after three consecutive classes—AP physics, Spanish, and European history—I felt completely drained. I laid on my bed in my dorm room. Maggie had told me that she was inviting some friends to our dorm room again for a girls' night. But I just didn't have the energy to talk anymore. I could feel my brain starting to act up again.
I decided to let go and be myself in front of her. We would do what friends do—share secrets.

I found myself telling Maggie everything. The truth about what I presumed was my mild bipolar disorder. My depression. All my brain issues.

She looked suspiciously at me. "Jiayi, do you mean you have bipolar disorder?"

"Yeah," I said. "Mild bipolar. Like mood swings."

She acted as though I hadn't said the word *mild*. "You mean like those people who get super depressed one day and crazy high the next?"

It didn't sound quite right, but I didn't know how else to describe it. I agreed.

"In that case," she said, "you probably need serious help. You should go to the school counselor."

She didn't invite her friends to our dorm that evening. Instead, she was away for the entire night. Something in my mind knew that I had made a terrible mistake by telling her the truth. The next day, she stopped talking to me all together. When I passed by her and her friends, I saw the cold stern looks in their eyes, as if they were seeing me for the first time. As if they could see through me. In addition to being a girl without enough natural beauty or a decent personality to make up for it, I was banished. And it had been caused by my worst enemy.

Me.

I had spilled the ugly secret out. I had told her who I really was.

They say the truth will set you free. Look where that got me.

13 Pink diary excerpt

I started therapy—by writing in a pink diary:

Time won't fly. It's like I'm paralyzed by it.

But time does fly.

Time does.

And it flies so damn fast.

It's like getting stuck in a spiral, like a hamster running in a wheel, again and again, spiraling. Somehow I know I will just dwell in this shit for a while and nothing will make sense for a very long time. And I will be rolling in the mud against all my will.

I don't know why God has put me down this time. I don't know if God will listen at all. God, will you listen? Why do you have to let me go through this? Am I your precious daughter as you said before?

Am I?

Sometimes I even wrote long letters to Maggie.

Why don't you show any more signs of liking me? Why do you have to do this to me andnow everyone else at school does? Don't you know that I would do anything for you? I mean anything? I will be the most supportive and loyal friend you would ever have if you would just show me that I'm a bit special? Don't you know how careful I have to be to not be hated by you? Don't you know that? Can't you hold me tight and tell me that you actually like me? Could you do that? Could you please do that?

I put down my pencil. Then I laughed at myself. *So stupid*, an inner voice remarked. *So desperate.*

14. Pink diary excerpt

Despite what they think of me or what I think they think, the only thing to do is to focus all my energy on academics.

The next few days, I will be bombarded with lonely days and nights. Friends won't be able to be who they are when they are with you because you can't be who you are when you are with them. Why does it feel so good with zero hours of sleep? As if the machine finally starts to run smoothly after long hours. But how long will it last? A transient moment, I figured.

She's trying to climb uphill with a large number of suitcases loading her down, suitcases that have been with her too long to get rid of.

If only I had no baggage. What kind of magical life would it be?
But she could never keep up a consistent pace.

Why are you stalling again? Are you afraid that others will know what being you feels like?
Why are you shaking with fear again?

Let's forget about you for a little while.

A quote from a reading jumped into my mind. *Humbleness is not thinking you are of equal or less position than others, it's not thinking of yourself at all.*

Okay, now you are so philosophical.

Just leave me, help me forget everything for a little while.

The cement floor felt like walking on flurry clouds.

I opened my eyes. I wasn't walking on clouds. I was in a room with knives and stainless steel countertops. I knew it was way past curfew. The problem was that I didn't know how I got here.

I heard a knocking. *Jiayi, open the door*, said a gentle female voice.

Knock, knock, knock. *What's happening in there? Why are you saying weird things to yourself?*

With a start, I realized that I was murmuring a million different words to myself. And then I recognized the room. I was in the dormitory kitchen.

My legs couldn't move. Seeing that I had been gone for a long time, Maggie had gone out to search for me. I started to realize that I was dreaming an illusion and tried to wake up. But my brain suddenly felt as heavy as a brick, dragging me straight to the bottom of the sea when I was trying to remain afloat. I fell on my knees trying to get myself up. An inhuman sound came out of my voice from the bottom of the throat. *Hey, your roommate is calling you. Hey, please wake up.* But my traitor brain kept sinking and sinking and an unbearable pain started in my stomach in my brain like repetitive electric shocks.

Please, someone help me. Someone who I know that it's okay to breakdown in front of. Someone who won't judge my pain.

More knocking. *You're scaring me, Jiayi,* said the voice.

I stood up. Suddenly I could move again. I calmly went to the door of the kitchen and walked out. The soft female voice belonged to Maggie, who looked relieved as I walked past her. I pretended that nothing had been wrong. Maybe I was too wrapped up in my own battles to see my roommate's efforts to connect with me again. Maybe all she wanted to ask me was to take down my guard and let her in my heart.

But I can't, Maggie. I won't allow it. I won't allow you the chance to judge me again.

15. Ice cream social

After our third ice cream cone, somebody got the bright idea of playing Truth or Dare.

Three days of being locked away in my dorm, and I had gone socializing with some new friends from my Spanish class. A girl had proposed the game. I always loved those types of moments because they brought something deeper out of everyone. The golden sunshine kissed me softly on my cheek and brought a huge grin on my face. It was a day when socializing felt as easy as a breeze, maybe because of the insane sugar high. Anyways, it was a day when I allowed myself to be whoever I wanted.

Ahhhhhhhhhhhh Louisa you lose! Louisa winked at me. It meant: *Okay, girl, ask any questions you want.*

Shuffling a million questions in my mind, I finally settled on one. "If you could choose to improve one feature about yourself, what would it be?"

I sat back and studied her face, wondering what Louisa would choose to alter. Her abnormally large face? Her swollen baby cheeks? Or her unbelievably crooked teeth? She never even used makeup, despite all the attractive girls who roamed the campus and got attention from both faculty and students. It was the time when both Louisa and I had begun to become conscious of our faces and bodies. Our English teacher, Mr. F, once joked to a gorgeous model named Sophia that he wouldn't allow her back in his class if she turned orange from her beach trip to South America. Making it worse was the fact that the boys were constantly ranking the girls based on their attractiveness and beauty.

Louisa looked pensive for a moment. Then she said,

"I wouldn't change anything. I think I'm good enough."

Her firm tone indicated that she was completely sure of her decision. How could anyone choose not to change themselves for the better when given a chance? Weren't we supposed to keep molding ourselves in life until we became perfect? How could anyone be a hundred percent content with who they were when they were not even close to perfection? I didn't understand. If I had a chance to change myself, I would have enlarged my almond shaped eyes. I would have added more color to my pale, lackluster face.

But Louisa seemed so confident and comfortable in her skin. There was something quite attractive about that. It was something different from the physical appeal of a person. The fact that she couldn't care less about her flaws made everyone around her see only beauty in her imperfections as well.

At this point, I began to have only two modes. Extremely happy or beyond depressed. I started to believe everyone had one mental disorder or another. They just were so much better letting it be. It was normal for a human being to be sad from time to time and amazingly happy the next minute, right?

I spelled it out in my pink diary.

Driver, please make a U turn. He doesn't make a U turn. I'm still heading in the same direction. The driver can't seem to hear a thing. He is deaf! Motionless! His poker face reflection in the front mirror scares me. *Please*, I beg, *turn around, I need to go down that happy road, not the depressed road.* Suddenly he turns around and stares at me. His motionless face turns green. He steps harder on the pedal, and drives full speed down the road to hell.

That is exactly what my version of what bipolar feels like. Trapped in a taxi with a crazed driver at the wheel.

16. Rong

I must have looked extremely odd at that time. I carried a large book-bag loaded with all my textbooks and notebooks. I wasn't even totally sure of the Kent dress code. I walked around in somewhat formal dresses on campus and avoided eye contact. In short, I tried every possible method to isolate myself.

Miraculously, though, I found myself drawing closer to a new friend.

Rong.

An extremely classy girl from a wealthy family, Rong was an excellent harp player who carried the aura of a princess.

As the relationship between my roommate and I slowly grew more unbearable, I overheard Maggie telling somebody that she wanted to move in with Betty, another girl whose roommate had been recently been caught shoplifting.

The very next day, I walked into the dining hall, and lying on the usually empty headmaster table was a huge array of objects. Cell phones, necklaces, purses, wallets, earrings, headbands, Sephora makeup boxes. Boss headphones. At the table, Maggie was looking through the objects.

"What is this stuff?" I said.

Maggie didn't answer. Instead, she suddenly lifted a necklace. "I found it!"

I watched Maggie squirm with happiness. I realized that these were the objects that Betty's roommate had stolen from everyone living in middle south girls' dorm. I was flabbergasted that she was able to hide all of those things in her tiny space of the dorm room.

"How did—"

"She got expelled," said Maggie, matter-of-factly.

Oh wow. It's good that she got expelled. A thought climbed into my brain. *What about you?*

Another voice poked. *You are nothing but a phony. You have a brain that changes itself every minute. You are unstable. Does Rong know? Will she still see you as her friend after she finds out the reality?*

Having a weird brain is not a crime, I answered. And now I was going to take a radical step that would improve my life. I decided to do both me and Maggie a favor.

"Hey Maggie," I said.

"What's up?" she replied, eyes still fixed on her necklace.

Her squadron of friends behind her giggled. Some looked at me suspiciously. Betty stood next to her as if she was ready to protect her friend from the bullets that threatened to shoot out of my eyes.

"If that girl got expelled, does that mean that Betty needs a roommate?"

"Yep."

I heard myself blurt the words. "Would you like to switch rooms?"

Maggie looked surprised. Then she looked confused. Then she became extremely happy. Showing me the first smile I'd seen in weeks, she agreed fervently, as if for a brief moment I was her friend again. Even Betty softened a little.

"Of course!" said Maggie. "We should go to the principal's office as soon as possible. Could we go today? Gosh, are they closing at five?"

It happened fast. Within a week, Maggie moved out, and Rong moved in. It was all for the best. I had made new friends, ones who would love me for who I was.
Friends that I would need to survive.

17. Meatless Monday

"Yuck. It's sushi again."
I looked behind me. At the end of the cafeteria line was a guy was wearing a Kent Hockey T-shirt. He was with two buddies who looked equally grossed out. They must have been day students as I had never seen them on the campus before.
I grabbed a plate and didn't pay them any more attention. After all, the fields behind Kent produced probably thousands of pounds of organic potatoes every single year, and the dining hall usually had something amazing for everyone. Even today, on meatless Monday, the amazing variety of mouth-watering vegetarian recipes was more than enough to satisfy our nutrition needs and taste buds.
For example, making a chocolate pancake at the self-serving pancake station was the single most important ritual to start my regular schoolday. Not to mention the cereal bar which had over 12

types of cereals and was available 24/7. Furthermore, the Korean kitchen staff would kindly give me extra plates of whatever I requested.

On meatless Mondays, most of us marveled at the sushi rolls, vegetarian burgers, and other dishes. I temporarily forgot the heavy baggage of mental issues when staring at those foods. Who knew vegetarian dishes could taste this amazing?

I assembled my plate of sushi and poured wasabi-flavored soy sauce generously on top of the rice. Then I heard a second voice.

"Yo," he said, "we have *games* today. We need protein. What the fuck is this?"

I looked backward. A third guy had leaned over the counter and was shouting to the Korean kitchen staff. "Hey. You. Could you make us some *steak*?" The staff shook their heads without saying a single word.

"Fine. Let's go." The three guys stormed out of the dining hall.

I sat down at a table and began to enjoy my succulent raw fish. A half-hour later, the same pack of students re-entered the dining hall. They were carrying three large brown McDonalds bags. They sat down at a table and laid out several Big Macs, large fries, and boxes of Mc Nuggets. Then they started devouring the food.

Our dean clearly was not pleased.

That night we got notice that our long-anticipated snow day had been cancelled. The dean later reported the behavior to the principal, who was definitely not happy.

No one ever ate meat on Monday again, at least not during lunch in the dining hall.

18. The Power of Now

Just surrender.

I stared at those words for a long time. I was reading a book that my mother had sent to me after having a moment of so-called awakening. It was called *The Power of Now*, by Eckhart Tolle.

Surrender? Me? That wasn't possible. If I surrendered, my world would truly collapse. Although I hadn't been able to make myself speak for the past four days, I refused to consider the possibility. I no longer had the shakiness in my brain, and there seemed no hope whatsoever for me to ever be normal again. The days in my dorm room were filled with lonely hours with my books.

Could this book change that?

Just like what the author Eckhart Tolle had written in the book, I could not understand those words on a mind/brain level. I tried to read passage by passage, word by word to make more sense of the material in front of me. My actions didn't want to follow the words. *Look at your thoughts,* the book demanded. I couldn't. There were thousands of thoughts going on at this very second, how is it impossible to watch them as an outsider?

The poster of Taylor Swift on the left side of my dorm began to bother me. It was too visible for my brain to bear, but the book kept demanding that I try to feel my body as much as possible.

Use your body to access the present moment. There lies the power. There lies your true being. My brain was still fixated on the objects around me.

Surrender. Surrender. Surrender. A sound with a rhythmic quality to it came to my body. The walls slowly fell down. They were made of tofu, anyways. All the battles for the past few weeks were unleashed and released.

I don't have to talk to anyone in Kent. If I don't want to talk, or if my mind cannot concentrate, that's perfectly okay, too. If my math counselor won't let me register for AB Calculus, I will stay in the regular calculus class. If no decent colleges will accept me when I graduate, I will return to my family. I don't care about a single thing anymore. Whatever will be, will be.

As soon as I raised the white flag, my enemies disappeared before my very eyes. I became infinitely larger.

The week following this temporary surrender after the battle was incredible. As if miraculously, people decided to like me. I enrolled myself in a hip hop dance class and made a new

friend, Sophie, who had a very nurturing energy that enabled me accept myself fully. Maggie still tried to avoid me but I didn't care anymore.

I had the Power of Now.

19. Marijuana

Despite the fact that I had never had sex or smoked marijuana, I actually managed to get myself a boyfriend.

His name was Bill.

A more than decent boyfriend. He went to a boarding school near Kent. He was tall, warm, and funny. The rules of finding a boyfriend were foreign to me, but when we met at a social event, we immediately clicked. He easily broke through my shell of shyness with his warmth of character. He liked me and was interested in anything I was interested in. We studied, went to the movies, and explored the town of Kent together. I never had to think of what to talk about when being with him. Conversations with him were easy.

Bill's regular trip to visit me quickly became a highlight of my week. For a brief while, I could forget about my problems and schoolwork and actually breathe. He taught me to enjoy simple intimacy. Holding hands and laughing while we walked across campus. He loved telling good jokes. I couldn't help but laughing hysterically after he joked about my mental problems (I had confessed everything to him) as being nothing but my imagination.

I had never had any serious relationships. For a girl who wasn't sure of herself, Bill's caring and love were somewhat reassuring. However, I decided not to have sex with him. He never pushed me, either, and he always stopped at the right time, as though my company alone was good enough for him.

Experimenting with drugs was a widespread secret at Kent. The school officially held that it was a serious crime. Students found possessing drugs period would be expelled. After all, Kent had a prestigious reputation to uphold.

The truth was that the school had a lingering drug problem that had only been addressed once or twice before, when the school was being sued. While the academic atmosphere might have been strong, it wasn't as strong as those at other top boarding schools that my friends from Harvard attended.

My first encounter with this subculture came through Brittany, a friend I made in the Spanish class. She asked me to go to a weekend party in the CASE dorm that her friend put together. It seemed like a regular dorm party, with homemade cookies, brownies, and tortilla chips. But later
that night, when Brittany signaled me to go outside to the corner near the river, something clearly wasn't right.

A circle of people I had never met were smoking pot. They looked suspiciously at me and muttered something about why Brittany had brought me there. *It's all right*, Brittany said, *she'scool*. As if Brittany had performed magic, all of them went back to their business. I feltuncomfortable among them. *Drugs are just wrong,* I heard myself say. I didn't know if I had just said it out loud.

They glanced back at me as if I had dropped a bomb in the circle. I guessed it had been out loud. A blonde girl, Tess, with dreamy brown eyes started giggling. I felt something very uncomfortable about her underneath her beautiful facade.

"Jiayi," she said, still giggling, "have you ever had sex with your boyfriend?"

I realized that they had all seen Bill. "Nope," I answered.

All the people were staring as though it were obvious that my values were wrong. Tess kept pressing. "Why not? How long have you been dating?"

This time, I kept my thoughts inside. *I'm only sixteen, Tess. I don't feel like having sex or experimenting with drugs, especially when I don't know what they could do to my already precarious brain. In fact, I'm much more interested in those tiramisu brownies.*

I didn't know how to refute her. They all seemed to know much more about life than me. All I knew was occupying my brain with academic work or trying to make new friends to prove my self-worth.

Brittany never brought me to another party again. As a matter of fact, she never talked to me in public, other than in Spanish class.

20. Dress Code!

"Could I have another chocolate pancake?" I asked.

In the spacious dining hall of Kent school, I watched the dining hall staff make another pancake for me. The thought of listening to another lecture by Mr. Stewart, my overly stern English teacher, had caused me to begin avoiding class. It didn't matter that I was already ten minutes late. My body wouldn't go.

When I arrived, he rolled his eyes. "You're late again."

"Sorry."

I didn't have any great excuses. Time didn't seem to be on my side. The shower always took longer than expected. Breakfast, too, because I couldn't stop eating. Finding our giant textbook in my messy pile of stuff took an additional ten minutes. I would forget my glasses. An hour before class felt like eternity, but it ran through my fingers like sand. I was never able to keep it.

His eyes roved up and down my outfit. "You're not even in dress code."

I nervously looked down at my black jeans and royal blue knitted sweater. I halfway heard him begin to lecture me about the importance of dress code. It's a matter of respecting the tradition and rules, he said. How could a student achieve anything in the future without knowing how to dress appropriately?

He had a point. Still, when he sent me back to the dorm to change clothes, I walked really slowly.

21. Why aren't you singing?!

Harvard, please take me back.

It was funny how long that dream was able to keep me emotionally afloat. Before my head drowned in the water, I truly believed in every cell of my being that I would find my way back to that gorgeous campus. I ignored the fact that the Harvard admission office cared about a candidate's personality first and foremost. I put aside the fact that for the past three years in a row, Kent hadn't been able to produce a single Harvard acceptance. I didn't have time to notice. I had to try despite my conditions and fears.

So I decided to try out for the school orchestra. I'd played violin for years, and I thought it would look good on the college application.

At the audition, I played Bach. The orchestra leader assigned me to the first violin section. That wasn't too much of a surprise. The surprise came when I auditioned for the school choir and was placed in the soprano section.

Good, said the voice in my head. *You're on your way to Harvard.*

With these new activities, my new schedule was punishing. Six main classes, two musical obligations, daily church duties, formal dinners, and countless other obligations. My life had some meaning by jamming it full of things.

But they also started to take a toll on me. There are limits to what a sane mind can handle, let alone an insane mind. As much as I enjoyed playing in orchestra and singing in choir, I started to appear fatigued, and it showed in choir. We had just finished a rendition of "Amazing Grace." Emily, the choir leader, stared at me.

"Why aren't you singing, Jiayi?"

"I am singing." It was true. I could hear my voice.

"No, you are not."

Everybody looked at me. It was the second time she had questioned me publicly during a rehearsal. Emily was not only the head of the choir, but also a senior. Being a senior meant that she had the power to give us "hours," the second-worst scenario next to being expelled. If she thought it was reasonable, she could make me spend hours cleaning plates in a dining hall, or picking up leaves from the grass.

Mrs. Moreno, the choir director and a highly skilled organ player, gave me an equally cold stare. "Jiayi," she added, "if you want to stay in this choir, you have to sing."

Feeling enough judgment from them, I decided not to anger them any further by defending myself. If they couldn't hear my voice, then I would sing louder. I couldn't risk getting myself kicked off the choir. It was the only activity that allowed me to connect with others without small talk or chatter. And I needed it to go to Harvard.

After the rehearsal, I headed into the restroom. Pushing the door open, I heard Emily's voice starting a rant. *Goddamn stupid Asian*, she was saying. Her voice had been so gripped by fury that she hadn't even heard me enter. I paused in the doorway, a huge question mark stamped on my brain. What had I ever done to her? We had never argued. I had never said a negative word about her. I had never harmed her in any way. I had no idea that I could be hated that fervently.

On the short walk from the chapel to my dorm room, the tears kept rolling down my cheeks. My *goddamn stupidity* had already placed me at the lowest point of social statuses. Then my dream of returning to Harvard started nudging me. *Don't be led down that road. You have other important things to focus on. This will pass. No big deal. Just a bad day.*

Then I remembered Eleanor Roosevelt saying that if someone can hurt you, it's because you let them.

And I still wanted to get into Harvard.

22. Piano Room

Sitting on the greasy carpet in a locked, four square foot, windowless piano room, lighted by my iPad screen, I blasted "Innocent" by Taylor Swift.

There's something you can't speak of, But at night you live it all again.

No one on the campus would come down to the music room at 11 p.m. Not even my skittish dorm parent, the thumb-headed math teacher watching over us that day, could have assumed I was there. The postage-stamp-sized piano room, hidden behind the hall we used for orchestra rehearsals, was the one place I could truly be alone and allow myself to *feel*. To process the overwhelming amount of stimulation from the day, the inessentials my brain couldn't filter out. This was where I connected to Taylor Swift's songs. It was liberating to have something to relate to, something that described exactly how I felt, as though I could finally pinpoint my emotions among the incessant shuffling of a messy card deck.

Guess you really did it this time
Left yourself on your war path.

Emily's bitter remarks in the bathroom were reflected in the beautiful song. My battles were getting harder, the monsters growing more unbeatable. Tears streamed down my face and the haunting guitar melody struck right at my brain.

Wasn't it beautiful when you believe in everything,
And everybody believed in you?

The loving smiles of Audrey, Shirley, Grace, Marisa, and countless others began flooding through my head like an Oscar-winning movie trailer, carrying a distant memory of being so easily loved by the world.

It's alright, just wait and see

Your string of lights are still bright to me.

Taylor Swift began raising her angelic voice. I hugged myself tighter. I couldn't wait forever for myself to get better.

'Who you are is not what you've been.' Aren't we all merely flesh and bones with a collection of experiences?

'There's something you can't speak of

But at night you live it all again.

You wouldn't be shattered on the floor now

If only you had seen what you know now

then…

That was it. I started weeping like a child. Hopeless, scattered in tiny pieces on the carpet. How I wished that it was all merely a nightmare. How I wished that my brain was normal enough to allow me to connect with these amazing people at Kent. How I wish they knew a different me— not this delicate, broken, indecipherable creature.

Wasn't it beautiful running wild till you fell asleep

Before the monster caught up to youo

Tears were flooding down now. I had to move the iPad screen from my lap to the piano keyboard. I felt an internal shift. A rejuvenation. A regrouping, a release of pain.

Times turns flames to embers...

Everyone of us has messed up too.

This powerful reminder finally ushered some sense into my mind, that had until that moment seemed defeated and hopeless. A sense of calmness and reassurance started to course through my veins. Maybe time does heal everything, like the lyrics in *Fifteen*, which my friends sang on my sixteenth birthday. I just had to live longer than the pain to witness it.

Life changes like the weather

Today is never too late to be brand new.

Could there burn an ember of hope in this impossible situation? I switched off the music and climbed out of the darkness. I walked out the back door of the music room, into an outdoor narrow passage, the shortest route back to the middle south dorm, my way paved with carpet leaves and weaves, all tangled up together along the sidewalk.

23. Diva

Beyoncé's sound blasted the Kent school dance class. Dancing awkwardly, I certainly didn't feel like a diva. I felt as though I was tarnishing Beyoncé's music. Her confidence and amazing stage presence made her so powerful yet so distant. I didn't deserve to dance to her music, let alone the song "Diva," which I was scheduled to perform in front of the entire Kent community in Mattison Hall.

I followed the footsteps of the director of the Kent school dance program, which embraced the world of contemporary dance. We could even choreograph our own dance. Next to me was a senior named Jane, who later was accepted to Johns Hopkins. She danced gracefully, much better than me, her lovely spirit shining through.

"Now look back," the director was saying, "and go there. And look back again." The team arranged itself into a V-shape.

"Jiayi!" the director yelled at me. "You are supposed to be *up front*."

The entire V-shape was led by me moving from the stage right to center stage. Yet my brain was too attached to the fact that I couldn't remember the previously complicated sequence to move to the next own.

"Ah, sorry," I said. Ashamed, my voice sounded so low.

The director rewound the music. Jane yawned and sighed.

The music started playing again. *I'm a diva. I'm a diva. I'm a diva.* I watched and copied Jane's movements completely as my brain couldn't recall a single previous movement.

Diva best believer. On cue, I jumped to the front. The entire team followed quickly and made a gesture that made us look like a sliding side card deck. The vision from the mirror was extraordinary.

"Good work," said the director. After two hours of rehearsing, we'd finally satisfied our overlord. Thank God.

I headed immediately to the dining hall and grabbed four brownies. A dorm friend had just taught me her invention of making "hot" ice cream by microwaving the brownie for exactly 30 seconds in the dining hall. It was so delicious that all the awkwardness during the day faded away.

I may not have been a great dancer, but I was great eater. Little did I know the role that food was going to play in my future.

24. The counselor

Bill urged me to talk to somebody—a counselor, a therapist, a neurologist, anyone who could help. His suggestion resonated with what I had wanted to do all along. I knew his loving intention behind the suggestion.

I went straight to the Kent school infirmary the next day.

I confessed everything to the counselor. Every shred of my ugly thoughts. My entire journey of going from being labeled as mildly bipolar to my unpopularity to my anxiety about Harvard.

The counselor paused for a while before she began to speak. "Jiayi, when did this all start?"

"I don't know," I confessed.

"Could you remember a time when you were happy with being yourself?"

I thought back. There were definitely times when I had been happy with myself. But never one hundred percent. After all, there had always been imperfections. There had always been things that I wanted to alter. I had always imagined what it would be like to be like other girls.

"You need to love yourself first," she said. Her eyes scanned my facial expressions and sensed my reluctance. "We will get you through this, but you need a lot of help."

Her eyes were filled with compassion. She recommended that I see a professional psychiatrist. Concerned with how expensive therapy would be, I started imagining the worst-case scenario. I could hear the psychiatrist's final diagnosis. *She's hopeless. Completely hopeless.* So far, nobody had been able to chase my dark demons away when I was severely depressed. And no one had been able to bring me back to earth when I felt powerful enough to dance across moonbeams. I might be forever swung by the whims of my brain.

What if I was beyond anyone's help?

25. Pirates of Caribbean

F you. You are an absolute piece of shit.

Standing in someone's front yard, Bill and I were throwing the worst possible words in the English language at one another.

He'd just travelled an hour by train to see me. And I'd bluntly refused to meet him. I'd figured that he must have been the source of the worsening of my problems, so I'd told him that I'd decided to break up. Because my brain had been stuck in the darkness, it had decided to tear apart my single wonderful relationship in the hope of bringing dramatic changes to the rest of the intolerable dilemma.

It didn't matter that he'd been the most perfect boyfriend possible, the sweet caretaker who hugged me when my brain became shaky. When I'd started ranting about myself, he'd reminded me how wonderful and special I was. He'd taken me hiking in the beautiful Berkshire Mountains. He'd bought me a bike and taught me how to ride along the most exquisite trails in the area. He'd ended all our dates by buying me a huge ice cream sundae. His visits to Kent were literally the only positive aspect of my bland existence.

Now I refused to speak to him.

A part of me knew I was being unreasonable and cruel. But my brain had decided the relationship was too much. My brain told me that he was distracting me from concentrating on academics and getting good grades. My brain told me that he was a devil in the guise of an angel, that he would eventually break up with me, that my problems were worsening every day.

So my brain made me do it.

It was so determined to betray me that there was no way I could hold on to sanity for much longer.

I watched him cry, listened to him curse. He didn't understand the reasoning. It was *better* this way. He would thank me someday. He would see that I'd allowed him to let go of this bundle of negativity and move on to more positive people.

Still, his tears melted something in me. What had I done? What if he would love me no matter how terrible I become?

No, I told myself, *he deserves better.*

26. Winter concert

Ka-chi, ka-chi. Hundreds of parents were snapping photos.

It was the winter concert.

Music events seemed to be happening all the time at Kent, but the winter concert was still the biggest event of the year. After Mrs. Hobbs assigned me to the first violin section, I started practicing regularly in the practice room behind the large rehearsal room. After all, practice makes perfect. It's the 10,000 hours rule, the credo of Asian mothers everywhere.

Our selection this year: A selection from the soundtrack to *Pirates of the Caribbean*. It had to be practiced to perfection. After all, it had an incredibly fast tempo, as well as a melody that livened up everything it touched. Rong, Jean, and I had practiced it incessantly.

However, one problem persisted. The quality of the sound my violin produced changed with my state of mind. And my state of mind was changing even more often than the weather.

One minute before the winter concert. I drew the bow across the instrument. *Laaaaaaa.*

The violin was screaming the wrong notes. I panicked.

"Rong, could you come help me?"

She moved away from her harp and started listening to my violin. "It's completely off charts."
The Pirates of the Caribbean was next. The violin one section had the portion with the fastest tempo. And since there were only six of us, every violin was crucial.

It's funny how my violin is fickle like my brain. When the sun shines and it's warm, the sound of the violin is fuzzy and sweet as chocolate. However, when it's humid weather, it squawks, a sticky and harsh sound like fingernails scratching on the chalkboard.

Before Rong and I had the chance to fix the first string, we were on. The leader of our violin section, Michelle, guided us to the stage. Although I was wearing a professional white blazer, I felt like a faker. I tried to avoid using the off-chart first string and used the third section of the third string. Things seemed manageable.

Until a sharp off-key note cracked. My violin partner looked at me, shocked. Seeing what had happened, he started to play louder and cover up for me on some sections. We moved on and cooperated from one note to another beautifully.

Afterwards, Michelle cheered for all of us. Even Mrs. Hobbs looked pleased.

I once read somewhere that the brain is like an instrument. When one string is broken, the entire symphony is ruined because of this one single mishap. Yet is it possible that the symphony would be just as beautiful with the right strategies and help? After all, the crowd was cheering. The proud look in Mrs. Hobbs eyes made her look even more radiant and sparkly.

27. Audrey's email

I wrote an email to Audrey:

America is so nice right now. My mom and dad came this week for parents' weekend and they loved it so much here! Kent was just ranked the most beautiful town in the U.S. during fall by Yankee magazine. We had conferences so they could meet all the teachers. Surprisingly, they all said I was great and praised me a lot. Yet classes are getting harder because some teachers agreed to put me in an advanced level.

Also, I performed in two concerts, one singing in choir and the other playing the violin. It was super awesome, as somebody said I dressed like a rock star.

Then we left the school and I stayed with them for four days. I went to a meeting with their Jewish clients. I went to Brooklyn in NYC and two Jews invited us to join them at a super ostentatious restaurant. We visited their JP Jewish clothing store in Brooklyn. It was so grand and luxurious.

I talked all the way back with a super smart Jew while mom and dad were sleeping. I truly learned a lot from him. Geez. You have no idea how smart and rich they are. It's quite hard to believe. He told me he does nothing for free. He also told me to treasure every moment in my life, and not to cry today but leave it to tomorrow. I guess that might be his key to his success. However my parents just left back to China today. I didnight y when we said goodbye but I cried hysterically afterwards.

Audrey replied with lightning speed. I was surprised she wasnas surprised considering the time difference.

Oh!!!! Parents weekend!!! They must feel so proud of you when they see you on the stage singing in the choir and playing the violin! Brooklyn with Jews—catch the opportunities to talk with wise people—they may change your life, sweetie!

And she moved on talking about her lovely life in Shanghai Foreign Language School.

I reread my email and realized that I had started to lie by omission. I hadn't told her everything. It was getting harder to tell people the truth about my life at Kent.

28. Manhattan cruise terminal

Negative thoughts only attract more negativity.

On that cold November night, I watched the cruise ship slowly pull out of port and disappear into the dark ocean. I sat miserably on my suitcase and put my head in my hands.

I had been scheduled to be on that ship.

I wasn't.

Thanksgiving break, and I was in New York. The cruise was bound for the Bahamas, and my mother was supposed to have been here. She was nowhere to be found.

While I waited in the Manhattan cruise terminal, I thought about my mother. I hadn't said no to her going to Brooklyn to meet her friends a mere three hours before the ship left, even though I'd had an aching feeling in my stomach that we wouldn't be able to catch the boat. But I couldn't say no to her. I could never say no to her, or an argument would ensue. So she'd left.

An hour before the cruise, she had called from Brooklyn, wailing that she couldn't find a cab. I immediately called an Uber for her, then walked around the cruise terminal, trying my best to negotiate with the cruise staffers. One staffer joked about how some people couldn't even be on time for a boat. Another staffer joked that he was going to make me twenty-one years old to get me on the boat solo. I explained the whole situation in clear words. My newfound ability to speak words clearly amazed me, since I hadn't been able to communicate with anyone for days.

After negotiating with the captain, the staffers kept the gate open an extra fifteen minutes, knowing that my mother was on the way. I began to pray for a miracle. An entertainer for the cruise rushed into the terminal and pleaded to get on the boat. I watched him fumble for his passport and prayed that my mom's face would appear. It never did.

Finally, the staffers told me that it was all over. *You can rebook for Miami. It calls there on Friday.*

The gate was closed. The snow falling outside the terminal was too painful to look at.

I had let my mom win out over my intuition.

Every part of my body started to disintegrate. It was as though my brain was too fragile to handle even one small setback. I couldn't bear one more minute. I took the train back to my school and ran into my room and ate every single thing I could find in the mini fridge. Food rushed to my side and became the strongest ally at that miserable moment.

I felt the black creature that had made his home in my brain. It was about to catch me very soon. *Please delay coming for a minute. Can't you see how miserable I am right now? No matter what terrible fate I had in the past would pass.* My breaths came in short bursts. *Please breathe.*

Don't forget to breathe. The brain was troubled enough, but even it didn't have control anymore. The black creature was controlling it. *I need to get away from her for a while. She's a complete disaster. She's making my brain issues worse and more terrible as time goes on. Maybe I'm better off just staying with myself.* I usually called Uber for mom and somehow she always ended up somewhere else rather than her designated destination. She was totally unreliable. *Leave her alone,* said the voice. *It's not her fault. You are a failure of nature. It's just a matter of time before you break down and the world sees who you really are.*

I could feel the thread that held me to my sanity growing even thinner.

The phone rang. The caller ID said it was my mother. I didn't answer.

29 Uber Driver

Welcome to Florida. It's seventy-five degrees Fahrenheit. Madam, look! There is your ship! Waiting for you!

The Uber driver spoke with exaggerated excitement. He was more excited than my mom and I, two haggard people who hadn't even slept two hours.

It was the day after Thanksgiving. My mom had insisted on flying to Florida to catch the ship at the last stop before it left for the Bahamas. She thought that this cruise could potentially make me happier. I needed it. The previous month, I had lost the ability to write any sensible words in my diaries.

As she predicted, I felt like getting my mind back on track the minute I stepped on the ship. I took a deep breath. It smelled like the ocean. I was happy at that moment. Who cared if I turned into a different person tomorrow? My mother was here. And my identity was at least consistent in the way that it was always changing.

The Norwegian Breakaway ship was three times as large as the Titanic. Its own kingdom, the ship was a wonderland of activities and 24-hour dining buffets. Unlimited fruits, meats, seafood, chocolate chip cookies, cheesecake, and a thousand types of other delicacies. I stuffed myself with chocolate and vanilla ice cream.

The adults on the boat, however, all looked a bit unhappy, and didn't really smile, except at the children. Watching them splash around in the water park was enough to bring a smile on anybody's face. Their joy was contagious.

It wasn't long before the darkness descended.

Within a day, my thoughts had grown extremely disorganized. I would start a sentence and couldn't remember what I had started to say initially. I wondered whether it had to do with the fact that I had eaten all day long on the ship. Five scoops of ice cream, two pieces of chocolate cheesecake, and a strawberry sundae for breakfast alone. After the initial sugar rush, I became depressed. I became completely disengaged from my surroundings. When you realize that you can't even communicate normally to your own mother, you know that something must be very wrong.

Finally, she dragged me from the sofa in our room out to the pool. I blamed her nonstop all the way. I just wanted to sit alone. Why couldn't she leave me alone?

But once I arrived in the sunlight, all the problems seemed to fade away. I could feel the healing power of the ocean. A huge smile spread across my face as I finally relaxed. My mother began to smile, too. For the first time I noticed that her beauty only increased as time went by. She was a force of nature, yet the way she carried herself was pure grace. She was the only person on earth who would never judge me. I'm only certain of that.

30. Group Skype

A long message from Grace popped up my phone.

Group Skype at 10 pm EST (Jiayi at Kent), 7 pm PST (Renee in Seattle, 8am Colombia ST (Manuela). Everybody in?

Sure! I replied enthusiastically. I needed this group Skype with my Harvard friends badly. At least the brutal day started on a positive note. Mr. Stewart's class at 9 a.m. sharp again. He would give me demerits if I was late. We had an afternoon practice on varsity swimming team, another school activity I had signed up for hoping to get in to Harvard. Formal dinner at night, where we were required to dress up and sit with our advisor in assigned seats after 40 minutes of chapel service. A lot of students purposely chose their campus job service during formal dinner so that they wouldn't have to sit through this.

See you during varsity swimming practice! Brittany smiled at me during the last period of the day.

Please don't go, my body pleaded. I curiously stopped searching for my swimming suit as Rong walked in the room, her slim physique staggering beneath several giant textbooks.

I went to the infirmary and lied that I felt sick. I must have looked bad because the strict school nurse bought my excuse without the normal checkup that accompanies every student who claims illness. I got an excuse note and was spared from the brutal training.

The next five hours went by peacefully. Rong and I went to the music room to play her harp that had just arrived. It occupied half of the piano room.

At 10 p.m., the familiar Skype music rang immediately when I stepped into the room.

Lulu, Grace, Manuela, Renee, Jonathan, Elly, and even Joos, the adorable French guy were all on Skype. I could barely hear them as the Intranet at Kent never functioned well. But seeing their faces made me so happy.

Let's play secret Santa this year! Grace said. We played an online game while chatting around and I got assigned to give Lulu a present.

Just as I was pondering what I could possibly give to Lulu, a genius who got 2380 on his SAT at age 15, who knows every global economic event by heart, my dorm parent, a math teacher, came knocking on the door checking on us. It was 10:30 p.m., bedtime. I was fully dressed and using the computer.

"Two demerits, Jiayi," The dorm parent scolded. "I'm very disappointed in you." The loud chatting noise on my Skype went silent. One demerit meant two hours of working on campus. "Go to bed now." The math teacher saw my Lowell House friends starring across the screen to him. "Or else your New York trip will be cancelled." I waved at my Harvard friends who had become utterly silent, and closed my laptop.

Not a day seemed to go by peacefully.

31 Headaches

Why does Kathleen have to sit so close to me? Why does Scott keep flicking the pen? Why is the classroom so dead silent yet there are thunderstorms going on in my mind?

I was taking an AP physics exam in a tiny classroom. Out of my left eye, I saw a classmate sitting to my left. My left eye refused to turn attention away from the girl back to the problem in front of me. The more I tried to convince my left eye to obey, the brighter the classmate seemed to shine. I tried to focus on the question.

An RC circuit is built using a 1.0M resistor, an initially uncharged 20 uF capacitor, and a battery with a terminal voltage of 5.0 V. Which equation would be used to determine the charge in Coulombs on the plates of the capacitor as a function of time?

It didn't make sense. None of the equations that I remembered could calculate this problem. My eyes start to hurt again. My left eyeball was already clenched tight, so I focused on the right one. Together, they were creating the most painful headache experience of my life. Then, suddenly something swelled up in my brain, and a sensation pushed relief through all of my brain. Immediately I felt calm. Although my left eyeball was still in that weird position, my mind was able to function again. I watched closely.

Maybe my body was much more intelligent than I thought.

32. Ms Z.

"You don't look good, Rosalinda.o

Ms. Z called me using a fancy Spanish name only reserved for her class. Ms. Z was a gorgeous Spanish teacher with model-like physique who could easily be mistaken as a Kent school student if not for those formal looking black blazers.

I hadn't eaten more than 500 calories a day for the last week. I saw online a girl's diary of losing more than half her weight on a strict 500 calories regimen. She even exercised at the gym every single day. For me, that wasn't an option, as the Kent school gym was always filled with faculty members and I was way too self-conscious to be seen agonizing on the treadmill. I chose to just drink tea on the 5th day.

"*¿Como estas?*"Ms Z said, greeting us.

"*Muy bien,*i someone answered.

"*Bien. Vamos estudiar algo muy interesante,*nteresanteiartudiargym wy tried to make us excited about what we would be learning on that day, Nonetheless, I felt myself starting to fade away. It was my sixth hour of class, and the lack of calories was affecting my judgment.

"*Perdón,*" I heard myself saying. *¿Puedo pasar al baño?*" Ms. Z seemed to be a bit startled as I walked out of the classroom before she replied anything. I took out a dollar and several quarters and bought a Coke in the vending machine nearby.

Just as the coke company advertisement said, I felt immediately alive after my blood sugar got ramped up by the sugary soda drink. The Coke also signaled the failure of a quick fix, my very first crash diet.
Bill came to Kent after class. We were supposed to go to the pizza garden for some greasy cheeseburgers and their signature golden fries. As the food came to the table, I watched Bill eat while sipping a soda. The junk food wasn't worth quitting my diet for.

"Aren't you going to eat anything?" Bill started questioning.

"Nope,o I said firmly.

After failing to get me to eat by ordering another chocolate mousse cake, he snapped. "When did you start to become so superficial?"

"What? What's wrong with wanting to be skinny?"an was confused.

"You are too skinny! Look how thin your arms are. It feels like one touch could literally break them."
I looked at my body. Who cares about arms? Most of the weight was on my stomach anyways. I had gone from a perfect 110 pounds to an apple shaped 130 pounds within four months. And during the past five days, I had already lost six pounds.

IJiayi. Please eat something. Do not starve yourself. You are not one of those girls. I didn't fall in love with a superficial girl."

I looked at him and wondered how it was possible to continue to love me after all that I had put him through. After how I had been then. Gaining 20 pounds in one semester and being a completely socially awkward person. Yet he still thought I deserved that cheeseburger, that milkshake, and that chocolate mousse cake.

Just when I wanted to use my last excuse of not being hungry, a sound that erupted in my stomach betrayed me. I started gorging the milkshake. Bill started lecturing me about how I only starved myself because of the utter lack of self worth. I felt happy for the first time in a while. It's amazing what delicious food and a person's genuine caring and reminder of your self-worth could do.

33 Audrey's email

Try to find some good people to talk to—and they will find you are really adorable!!! Honest!!!
—an email from Audrey

Yea. Right. I closed the email. I will let Audrey keep thinking that. I'm nowhere close to being adorable.

That Saturday, Mrs. Hobbs, our music director, decided to take some of the violin section members to a local health care center to play Christmas carols for elderly people.

During the ride, Mrs. Hobbs kept gushing about their family's plans for Christmas. I got to thinking about Santa Claus, about how the truth is hidden from children. At least, all of them except Mrs. Hobbs' adorable nine-year-old daughter Gracie, who loudly announced, "I know the truth about Santa Clause. Then she winked at us, saying that she would connive with her mom to keep the secret from her little brother John at all costs. The witty Hobbs children were among the most adorable visitors on the Kent school campus. The inner joy of the faculty children lit up the cold campus.

After an hour of driving, we finally arrived.

"Jiayi, what a surprise!"what a my violin teacher. She spotted me the moment we walked into the facility. She came to join the ensemble as well. She hugged me tightly.

The facility seemed thrilled that the Kent school orchestra had come all the way to play for them. Afterwards, they kept claiming how much they enjoyed our violin ensemble version of Christmas carols.

We played "Joy to the World," "Silent Night," "White Christmas," and wrapped up the performance with a fast-tempo "Jingle Bells." Just one day earlier, the battles with my brain had been getting increasingly intolerable because of my endless preparation for upcoming finals. Yet my mental drama completely stopped during this event, especially after an elderly woman kissed my cheek and told me I was adorable.

All my problems seemed much lighter when my heart was aimed at helping others.

It was such a wonderful day, I wrote back to Audrey. *I can't wait for actual Christmas.*

34 Christmas Break

Jiayi where the f are you?

My brand new iPhone 4s was ringing like crazy. I already had nine missed calls and three new text messages. *We are seeing the new Harry Potter film at Regal Cinema.*

Regal Cinema, Christmas break.

Ritz Carlton.

I had no idea my friends in Kent had booked the Ritz Carlton for our planned Christmas break in Boston. Wasnz that where all the successful business people stay?

My phone pinged again. A message from Bill: I'm in Boston.

A hundred thousand exclamation points sprang into my head, a hundred more than what Audrey used in our email exchanges.

Bill had just travelled all the way from Kent to Boston by train. But our statuses on Facebook said "single."

It was an operatic relationship. Wetrain. But our status ble. ," and wrapped up the performance with able. appy fo

Don't go out, even if he comes. So suggested a friend in our Christmas Ritz Carlton group. You will get us worried if you spend more alone time with him. You will end up going back to him.

The group echoed that advice. But my heart wanted something else. My heart needed tender loving care that my rich boarding school friends couldn't fill. But I couldn't bear the thought of being banished from one more group of friends I made at Kent, so I didnrding school

Instead, I sent an emergency VIP email to Audrey about the situation. As usual, from the other side of the world, she replied instantly, in all capitals:

OF COURSE MAKING FRIENDS IS A VERY IMPORTANT PART OF YOUR LIFE, BUT DON'T CONSIDER IT A TASK. YOU ARE SO AMAZING THAT FRIENDS WILL COME TO FIND U, BUT JUST REMEMBER TO BE OUTGOING AND FIND MORE STABLE FRIENDSHIPS!!! IT'S QUITE NORMAL TO BE ALONE IN HIGH SCHOOL SOMETIMES.

I couldn't read another word. I stepped outside of the hotel and there was Bill, waiting for me curbside with his luggage and bike. We got back together that afternoon. And, surprise, broke up again. Our on-off relationship became even more dramatic than a soap opera.

Fifteen days later, the turbulent Christmas break came to an end, and I crawled back to Kent.

35 dr. Kay

"Hello, dear," said Dr. Kay, "I heard from Mrs. Johnson that you weren't feeling very well?"

I nodded. "I can't concentrate very well."

"How so?"

I pointed to a lamp. "An object like that will jump into my sight and I won't be able to finish my studies."

He made a small *hmm* sound. "How many courses are you currently taking?"

"Six. And three of them are AP courses."

The psychiatrist sounded surprised. "You're a sophomore?"

"Yes. I tried to enroll in AP Calculus but Professor Michael insisted on keeping me in regular calculus class. I think he hates me."

"That probably isn't true. Too many AP classes might be a challenge for anyone. From what I heard, most students only take AP courses when they are juniors or seniors."

"Not if you want to get into an Ivy League school," I said. "You need to finish at least ten AP courses before graduation."

"I can see where the pressure come from. What other symptoms are you experiencing other than not being able to concentrate? Are you making any friends at school?"

"I have two friends now, but I'm a bit secluded. I don't get along that well with any other of my schoolmates."

"Two best friends sound like quite a promising start to me. From what I can see, you are a very bright young woman who might be too fixated on academic achievements and outcomes."

"Oh."

"You see, Jiayi, sometimes when you let go of thoughts about final grades, you get better grades as a result. Don't you feel that way sometime?"

I couldn't understand why our conversation just got diverted from my mental issues to my grades. He must be a phony. He doesn't have any way of helping me. I've seen psychologists like that. They don't believe that I'm actually ill because they don't understand.

"Yes, I feel like that sometimes. Thank you for your time, but I have to leave now. There's a violin rehearsal in half an hour on campus."

I left the therapy room without another word, leaving a startled Dr. Kay, wondering what he had done wrong.

36 Cacophony

"If I could open my brain to see how it works," I said, "I could insert a computer chip to bring it back to normal. How marvelous would that be?"

I was talking to my cousin, who I hadn't seen in months. He was in the Air Force now. His nonjudgmental presence and cheerful outlook toward the world made everything easier. No matter how shut down I was to the rest of the world, he always had the ability to open my heart and tell the truth.

"What if someday we can monitor our brain and bring it back to the moment that it decided to crash?"

After listening to all my weird thoughts, my cousin simply said two words:

"It's impossible."

I sighed. My brain had reached the pinnacle of frequent anxiety attacks during the last month. Especially when some important tasks came up that depend upon a well functioning brain, my brain chose to slam the door harder.
One thing worried me immensely. I'd become unable to play the piano.

A skill that I had practiced since age four was forgotten overnight. No matter how hard I tried, I couldn't use both hands anymore. It was as if the creature in my brain had decided to untie the knot between the left and right hemispheres.

This was alarming. At age seven, I had been able to play any melody after a minute of looking at the sheet music. At age 14, I learned Chopin's "Revolucionario," one of the most difficult piano pieces ever written, after going through standard piano tests three times. Yet at age 17, my hands had decided to no longer collaborate. Individually, they could play the keyboard on their own.

But together, they created a terrible cacophony.

"I don't need my brain to be superhuman," I said to my cousin. "I just want to be able to play piano again."

37. !!!

I got a movie role in Nanshenjiali!

It was an email from Audrey. I was shocked. Nanshenjiali is a high-budget movie edited from Qing-wenjun's novel, a highly acclaimed author from Taiwan. I couldn't believe my eyes.

And I'm coming to Yale University for a Model UN competition. Audrey continued. *BTW I've been doing those disgusting geographic questions and I now know I'm in eastern 8 time and you are in western 5 time! Oh my geographic exam. I WANT As!!! I MISS U!!!!!!!*

As usual, a hundred exclamation points in a single email. Her genuine enthusiasm and love of life never ceased to amaze me.

A month later, I met Audrey in New York. She jumped towards me and yelled, "I won the Best Delegate at Yale!" We celebrated this amazing news by buying as much candy as we wanted in Times Square.

While we were on the Toys ile ws rides, she looked at me. n ow's your life in Kent going?"

In the past, I had always told her the truth. But every time, in emails I couldn't help but give a more positive angle on the utterly intolerable situation at Kent.

This time, I lied completely. I really couldn't take any joy away from her. After stating repetitively how happy she was to see me, she returned to Yale University to take the SAT at the cost of missing the final debate.

And I boarded the next train back to Kent.

January 22nd. A Saturday. But it didn't feel like it. At all.

38 Pink Diary Excerpt

As the weeks went on, my thoughts grew even darker. I began to pace my room, delivering imaginary speeches to all the people from whom I felt alienated.

The more you love Jiayi, the more she will love you. Right now, because she doesn't feel any love from you, she has to blame her brain for her misery. If she doesn't point the arrow at something, she will point it at herself. Even better, pointing it at the people around her is a thousand times easier. Shoot, shoot, shoot—she will shoot all of you who are suspected of the crime of judging her. She will kill everyone who dislikes her. In her impending apocalypse, the world doesn't have room for those people, not a single one of them.

Don't you understand? Maybe the only shit this brain is able to produce is fairy tales, conjured out of thin air. Her brain feels trapped by her physical body. It's not who she really is, yet the darkness keeps taking over. Jiayi gets lost in the mud. When she's covered in mud, she thinks she is the mud. And the moment she thinks the thought, she becomes the mud.

Then I would realize that I was speaking to a mirror.

39. An angel

Midway through a three-hour long staring contest with my textbook, I felt the archangel tap me on my shoulder.

A million historical tidbits were scurrying around my head. *Queen Elizabeth I. Philip II. 1839. Mary Stuart. Protestants. The ideal Renaissance man.* The AP European History exam was in three months. Although I was only permitted to take regular European history as a sophomore, I talked my advisor into agreeing to enter me into the AP exam. I figured that since

I didn't have that many extracurricular activities to show off on the college applications, overloading my applications with an impressive number of AP exams might be able to do the trick.

Then again, I overestimated the limitations of my brain.

After hours of studying, the information only scratched the surface of my brain. Even with Mrs. Houston, an utterly amazing woman who inspires and uplifts everyone around her, a woman who changes the entire ambiance of a room, the amount of information on the exam was still unbearable. I tried to use note cards to study but then decided writing down information was too much work. So I started to use the flashcards app on my phone to download some of the flashcards on Quizlet. But unless I design my own study guides, I am unable to memorize anything.

So I opened my textbook again, desperately trying to absorb the information. And desperate times call for desperate measures. I decide to use strategies. I start to categorize all the events into smaller pieces. World War II gets divided into Germany/Japan, overseas colonies, Holocaust, etc. It's the era of the history material that I hated to study the most. It's too recent.

Too fact-based. Too bloody.

After spending another half hour joggling down facts and battling with the increasing shakiness in the brain, I was screaming inside for help.

That's when I felt the tap on my right shoulder.

I had learned in theology class about the angels and deities that God has created to help us. In fact, I'd always felt a connection to the Archangel Gabriel. As a little girl, I had even wanted to change my name into Gabriella. And all the Bible verses regarding this powerful being caught my attention.

When it happened, I nearly jumped out of my seat. Then an emerald green aura began to hold both sides of my brain, as if it were something precious, as if it could be fixed instantly. The image caught my breath. I looked at the textbook again, at the messy highlights and notes around the margins of each page—all evidence of my insanity—and something inside the brain opened. I saw dark clouds in the left rear part of my brain being lifted up. Then I heard someone say the word *breathe* loudly. I started to exhale.

Without hesitation, I turned back to the Renaissance, to the names and work of Renaissance artists. *Michangelo painted the Sistine Chapel. Coppo di Marcovaldo painted the Madonna delBordone. Cimabue created Maesta of Santa Trinata.* Information flowed out my brain like thewater out of a faucet.

It was Archangel Gabriel who had turned on the faucet.

The daunting amount of information suddenly seemed manageable. It became clear to me that giving the right attention to the most useful information was all that mattered. After another three hours of sitting in the dorm room, I realized that I had already read six chapters. Afterwards, my roommate Rong told me that she had never seen me concentrate for so long. I almost told her who had made that possible, but I didn't want any judgment.

Something is bigger than us. I couldn't let my mind block my way of accessing it.

40. Nietzsche

Please describe Nietzsche's main views about death.

I loved reading about Nietzsche. At that point, however, I just didn't know how to write about him, or about anything. Period. It was like my personal box of analysis and creativity had been forever locked by my brain. The fingers could still move, but the material couldn't exude out of them. The fingers could only produce the type of writing that would get a C.

I looked at the prompt again. *Please describe Nietzsche's main views about death.* I decided to at least try getting an A on this essay. I have too much respect for that philosopher to get anything less.

One word at a time. Rather than stressing over whether I had used the words right constantly, I just allowed myself to write anything that came to the mind. As long as the spelling was correct, there was no should or should not, good or bad, right or wrong. Once I set my mind free, my brain signaled my fingers to remove all restrictions. Rather than using an ideal tone of a imaginary skilled writer, I started interpreting Nietzsche's ideas in my natural writing voice. I didn't have to be perfect to write. I just had to be myself.

Dr. Greene gave me an A on the essay. He commented: *The way she treated writing was likecrafting artwork. Watching her write was pure joy.*

I was surprised. It's amazing what we can do when we set ourselves free.

41. On Fire

It's on fire!

Ding ling ding ling ding ling...

The unbearable noise woke me up from an unforgettable dream. A gigantic spaceship, stunning and marvelous, had been waiting for me to board. But the noise had screwed everything up.

Our dorm parent, the usually calm math teacher, hectically knocked on the door. eRong and Jiayi,and Jiayiiayiockake up and get out NOW!"

Rong immediately jumped up. I had no choice but to leave my warm bed. I grabbed a blanket and scurried out with her.

The hallways were filled with people—htudents, faculty and kids. The dorm parent showed us a path from the back door of the dorm to the St. Joseph Chapel. There was a lingering smell of smoke yet no signs could be traced to it. It seemed odd. It didn't even seem like a usual false alarm.

The girls were standing in St. Joseph Chapel. Wearing pajamas and flip-flops and sleep masks, they looked quite different without makeup and nice clothes. Yet every one of them wore the emotion of anxiety facing the uncertain situation. It was the first time in forever that the entire school had been forced together in the chapel in the middle of the night.

Suddenly the already dim lights in the church went dark. Some students started to panic. Then the lights turned back on, much brighter than before. Then we saw something extraordinaryhpiles and piles of toilet paper splashed around the church. The chapel organ was covered with bright colored paint. The chairs surrounding the sculpture of Jesus Christ were all scattered and some were placed on top of one another.

It was a senior prank.

Feeling tricked but relieved, we were more than ready all to go back to our warm beds. I wondered whether that spaceship was still waiting for me to board.

Yet the faculty blocked the door. They signaled us to all sit down. Father Schell, the headmaster, walked in. He looked solemn. He had come immediately from his house several miles away.

I hope you all know that this isn't a light matter. He was speaking as if someone had passed away. Then he urged anyone who knew inside information speak up. He said the local police would get involved investigating this matter as actual smoke and blaspheme of the church were involved. Apparently this prank had gone way too far.

Then more faculty members made impromptu speeches. More students started speaking up. Around 5 a.m., we were finally allowed to go back to our dorm.

I collapsed on my bed. I didn't know how to survive another full school day with only three hours of sleep. It seemed to be never-ending.

42. 'cheater'

Five days to my seventeenth birthday, I was more than ready to take one AP down. Unlike other AP subjects, this one felt super easy.

AP Psychology.

The most frequent and psychoactive drug in United States is a. Marijuana b. Cocaine c. Alcohol d. Caffeine

Easy one. The first part of the exam went even more smoothly than I expected. I finished an hour-long section in half an hour. I looked at all the seniors around me thinking intensely and felt more positive about myself. I was going to get a 5 on this one.

The proctor announced break time. I went to get water in my schoolbag. *Pick me up. Pick me up!* It was the pink diary, lying in the bag, speaking to me. Although I didn't see the point of carrying the diary to use the restroom, I followed the order anyway.

The long lines waiting for the restroom gave me headaches. But the pink diary clutched to my side felt like a best friend reassuring me everything was okay.

I returned to the room.

The proctor looked at me, wide-eyed, when I returned. "when I returned. at "Umm. Yea. It's no biggie. I didn't even look at it while I used the restroom."

"Like hell I believe that." The proctor shocked me with his scorching remarks. "You were cheating."

"No, I swear, I wasn't!"

The proctor's loud voice gathered even more teachers and seniors. Everybody was watching me.

"Mr. S, I didn't look at the notebook. Besides it's not useful." He seemed to be quite reasonable. He would understand.

"You really expect me to believe that you carry it to the bathroom?" Mr. S studied my face intensely.

I couldn't utter a word. How could you explain to an esteemed faculty member that you have voices put in your head by random objects? "I didn't know we couldn't take stuff outside during the break."

"You are not getting away with this one, Jiayi. You cheated." Mr. S put extra spite on the final sentence. The death sentence.

Free response time! 50 minutes left till the exam. Another proctor shouted, and the seniors scurried back and forth. *Go back to your seat and finish your exam, Jiayi, we will discuss it later.* My AP psychology score was cancelled. The College Board didn't even give me a chance to see the final score. The worst part was, I really didn't cheat.

43. Running away.

I opened up the email. It was from office of admissions at Kent and was addressed to my father.

Mr. He,

We must get the EA back with the tuition due in order to save a place for Jiayi for the upcoming term. Fax or email it to me as soon as you can or by the end of the week. If we do not hear from you, we will assume Jiayi is not returning to Kent, and we will offer her spot to a student on our waiting list.

Regards,

Teri

Ms. Teri F

Enrollment Administrator, Kent School Admissions

I immediately wrote back to Ms. Freeman before my dad had the chance to read the email:

Dear Ms. F

Sorry to inform you this late, but I have decided to transfer to another school. Please give my spot to the student on the waiting list.

Thank you,

Jiayi

44.

I decided to run away before telling my parents. On the plane ride back to Shanghai, I repeatedly told myself to never forget the time I had endured in Kent School. There was no way I could ever let myself go back to that place again. However, there was no one negative thing that I could really pinpoint. After all, it was one of the prettiest campuses on earth. What forced me to leave and never look back was my twisted perspective and the sudden worsening of my condition.

On the car ride from the airport to home, I revealed this news to my parents. One minute, my dad was expressing how happy he was to finally see his little girl. The next minute, his face turned green. He almost lost control of the car.

"What did you do?" he said.

"I can't go back to that place, Dad. I just can't." My dad always spoils me, but this time he looked genuinely angry. He kept yelling that he didn't care about the $50,000 tuition each year. What he wanted was to see me in a prestigious environment where I could be surrounded by intelligent and bright people. My mom started yelling, too. She complained about how hard it would be to transfer to another boarding school as a junior without a clear explanation. She pointed out that I had chosen Kent despite having many other amazing offers. And she scolded me that I let my mental problems cloud my judgments. And insisted that she didn't raise a quitter.

"You both have no idea how difficult this year was for me. How could you yell at me for something that you don't even understand? Besides, I have an entire summer ahead to figure out where to go next year."

I started crying. The car went dead silent.

The rest of the drive felt like eternity. After we got home, I dragged my luggage directly up to my room. I didn't even greet Harry, our German shepherd, when he jumped up and down, waiting for a pet.

I lay down on my bed. It was so nice to be in the room filled with teddy bears, stuffed animals, and that human-sized Mickey Mouse that has lived in my bedroom forever. It was a brief moment of peace. For a moment, nothing mattered. Not Kent, Not the fifteen-hour tortuous plane ride. I was home again.

My mom knocked on the door. She opened it and suggested that I enroll in the college preparation program at the University of Melbourne. It would be much cheaper for me as a permanent resident to go there since my parents had already decided to emigrate to Australia. I shrugged it off. I couldn't go to Melbourne. I couldn't be the balancing force for them anymore. It was a daunting task enough to have to contain my erratic brain. I had long lost the ability to bear any more family drama.

And there was no way that I could let them see how bad my actual condition had become.

45. The Seattle program

A large posterboard caught my eye during my SAT preparation in a tall building on Nan Jin Rd, the most hustling and bustling street in the already overpopulated Shanghai.

Earn your high school diploma through HS completion program. Receive a high school *diploma and college associate degree together in two years!*

Just when I had no idea where to go after Kent, God or some other higher power had led me to this sign. My superstition and blind faith once again prompted me to go check out what this was about.

I walked into the building and used the elevator behind the sign. The office looked like it was a combination of an English language teaching facility and an exchange student program.

I timidly asked the busy receptionist. tCould you give me some information about the sign outside your office?"

"What sign?"

"The high school completion program."I wasn't even sure there existed something like this in the world. Maybe they made an error after all. There's no way that I could go to high school and college at the same time.

"Oh yeah. Go to that office."She pointed at the door on the right."Go talk to Reagan. He will share more information with you."

I walked directly to Reagan, a warm and seemingly kind man.

I repeated the question. When I mentioned the word high school, he jumped right in and finished my sentence. "It's a high school completion program at North Seattle College. It's a fast-track study program that will enable you to transfer to another college after you earned the Washington state high school diploma. Many of our students have transferred to UCLA, USC, University of Washington, and the like. It's really an amazing program and all you need is to submit transcripts from a previous high school and a TOEFL score. Seattle is also a very suitable city for foreign—"

I interrupted him as if I were last minute apartment hunting. "ast minute aparReaganseemed surprised by this quick reaction but I didn't need any more sales pitch. I just needed a place to stay, to be, to continue high school, to make me feel like living.

I gave all the requested documents to him on that same day and in two weeks, I was accepted.

One week later, I was in Seattle.

46. Gucci

At the door, a little bulldog puppy came greeting me. "His name is Gucci," said a brown-skinned Philippine woman.

I had arrived at the home of a local family in Seattle. We had been introduced by a host family agent (yes, it is a real job) after registering myself in a high school program in North Seattle College.

The woman was my host mother, Norma. She had already laid dishes on the kitchen table. Ben, my host father, had the kindest smile I have ever seen. He made me feel immediately at home. And Gucci was one of those creatures that was beautiful and ugly at the same time. The couple struck me as those rare breeds of people who thought of others before themselves.

The house was comfortable and neatly decorated. In fact, the only gap between the living situation and perfection was the fact that the bedroom was located in the basement. According to the principles of feng shui, living in the basement brings bad luck. But things couldn't possibly be worse than they had been at Kent.

The newly found freedom felt more than liberating. Other than the times that I would show up in the upstairs kitchen occasionally, neither Ben nor Norma would see me. I could allow my brain to go insane without their notice. I could cry without worrying about somebody hearing me. I could allow my brain to alter itself. Because nobody would care and nobody would notice.

Still, Norma cooked five-star cuisine every single day. They regularly took me out for buffet dining. Their kindness was like a beam of light shining in the rainy and damp Seattle. And their niece Sophie, a girl born looking like a movie star, livened up my life.

Seattle. It was the first city that I had to make my way through, alone, with my brain. Despite that, I decided that I have to make some plans for the future. Some tangible, workable ones.

47. The Psychic

"You really need my help," said the psychic. "I see something very dark in you."

"You do?" I said.

"Yes, and I'll give you a reading for $25." She may have sensed my hesitation. "If you don't let me help you, you will be depressed and dark as long as the curse is there."

Her name was Dianne, and I was sitting in the weird room where she did her readings. I handed over the money. She closed her eyes, then opened them.

"All the misery in your life," she said, "exists because of a curse that was placed on you by your father's previous lover. It occurred while your mother was pregnant with you."

"Really?" I said.

She nodded, then said the name of that lady. It sounded awfully similar to the name of my dad's previous girlfriend, who had been one of his nurses. The psychic insisted that the curse had gone through my mother's bloodstream and impacted me. The nurse, Dianne said, didn't like my mother because my dad had chosen my mother instead of her. The psychic said that the curse had been leaching good luck from me ever since.

And she told me that she needed a lot of money to use large candles to burn the curse off.

Then she put something behind my seat and murmured her hope this will work. I thanked her profusely as I thought those were things that would chase my depression away.

At the time in Seattle, my mental craziness had reached its pinnacle. With the Seattle rain and zero close friends, I found myself crying a lot. I was lonely, anxious, and hopeless. Dianne had given me the most precious commodity: hope. I was thrilled that someone might understand, and even had the ability to chase away the darkness.

A part of me felt so relieved. As if something else were responsible for my brain problems. As if I were perfectly innocent.

On my second visit, Dianne took my hand. "You can't tell anyone about these sessions. If you do, it will deeply interfere with the spiritual work I am doing."

"Okay," I said.

Then she told me that she wanted to pray for me, and that she needed to buy special candles to do so. By burning the candles, she would be able to find out specifically what kind of curse was on me, and how it could be removed. I was thrilled.

Then she asked me to go to the ATM to withdraw eight hundred dollars.

"Eight hundred dollars?" I said.

"They're really large candles," she explained. "Black ones. They're quite expensive." She sounded very serious. I was embarrassed about the entire situation, so I kept it to myself anyway. I went to the bank and withdrew eight hundred dollars.

The next time I saw Dianne, she told me that the bracelets that the nurse had used to stage the curse had been very powerful. To counteract their strength, she would need to buy a Rolex. While I didn't see how this would work, her seemingly genuine concern touched me. I was still skeptical. Reading me, she said that she knew that what goes around comes around. And she had children and wouldn't ever do anything bad to hurt them. That sentence alone gave me reason to trust her.

I was utterly naive.

The next day, she told me that she had successfully lifted the curse. Then she showed me the type of Rolex watch that she needed to get in order to lift the curse completely. And then she gave me three hours to get the watch.

I dutifully spent the entire afternoon gathering thousands of dollars from my different bank accounts for her. Then we went to the Rolex store together. She had instructed me to say nothing to the people behind the counter except that it was a surprise for my mom's birthday. And she pretended to be my mom's best friend.

I bought the Rolex.

Writing this now, I still can't believe how stupid I was. But at least I'm able to talk about it. It draws a very unhappy feeling from the inside out.

One day, during class, I couldn't hold onto my story anymore. So I told a friend about the psychic. She was mortified and asked me to stop. "She's only using you as an ATM machine," said my friend. Then she showed me an article about a very similar trick.

I realized that I had been scammed. I began to panic. By that time, I had already given the psychic more than twenty thousand dollars. She had even called my mom and asked her to transfer another thirty thousand dollars because of my supposed situation. The psychic claimed that she could help our entire family, not just depressed little me. I knew that money was gone forever, because I didn't have any evidence. Dianne had made sure that all the receipts and payments were in cash.

Three days later, she called me, claiming to be sick in the hospital. She'd been burned by the process of removing the curse, she said, and she needed more money to heal herself so that she could continue the process. I told her that I was busy with finals and didn't have time to come.

The next day, her daughter called me. She yelled at me, accusing me of leaving her mom all alone. She threatened me: *If you don't get your stupid ass here, I will follow you around.* What a bluff. I felt like a bullied child, all alone in another country with nobody to lean on.

I wanted to give her a huge speech on how horrible it was to prey on people at vulnerable times. But I didn't. And over twenty thousand dollars had simply disappeared because of my mistake. My parents' hard-earned money had vanished.

In the end, I realized that I wasn't even angry with her. I was angry at myself for being a complete pushover and let someone else convince me of this crafted story that I knew was bullshit.

I can't even explain how it happened. I just know that it will never happen again.

48. Holbrook news

I was eighteen. During a high school reunion party, he approached me, a familiar face, yet still mysterious. A towering, handsome exchange student from Sydney, Australia. His dark brown eyes sparkled as though there were lights behind them. His sweet smile showcased his kindness and drew people to him. I had known him since I was 11, yet our circles had never intersected (exchange students had their own, nationality-focused circles). In the bustling city of Shanghai, we spent that Christmas wandering around the bund, shopping hand-in-hand and attending every Christmas party we were invited to. With the severity of my mental illness, I never expected anyone to recognize any issues beneath the surface. But even with my mind drifting off every ten minutes, he pursued me, though he never fully realized what was in store for him.

The trip was supposed to release mounting stress before the start of the first semester at North Seattle College. It was supposed to be a reward from my long-distance boyfriend, his coming all the way from Australia. Instead, it set loose on me and him and the world all my problems. It untethered years of inert emotions and exposed the worst parts of myself, things that I didn't want to expose to the *one person* I sought to impress. It revealed to Jason that he had fallen in love with a socially awkward, confused, anxious, and insecure girl. That trip, in my mind, became the breaking point of our relationship. The perfect image shattered in his head, the image of a girl with a big heart morphed into one of a scared, unsteady little bird. I didn't know how to love myself, while expecting and yearning that someone else could show me.

Honolulu

I accidentally read his diary. He's sleeping. He wrote that he has kept his jet lag going on purpose so that he could have more "alone time." I nearly *broke* down. I guess I'm with myself now. I have to do anything to love myself from this point forward. He must have had enough *of my drama, my extreme eating habits, my insanely short attention span, and my million other flaws, all created by this inner monster in my brain. Reading his diary has torn a part of my soul that carries the last shred of the possibility of being loved by the world again.*

Like a bowl of cold sticky-rice, a million little pieces stuck together in my brain, impossible to break apart. Thousands of emotions tangled up: resentment, fear, anger, self-loathing, confusion, worry, self-hatred. I started crying and punching myself in the head. The ever-present shakiness in the back of my left brain seemed to break apart a little. Blood started gushed from my nose. How could any human being be this *horrendous?* How could anyone love someone like me?

If all of this craziness is caused by the shakiness in my brain, will there ever be a cure? Probably not. What if I have to live like this for the rest of my life? I will never have the chance to be appreciated by others. The shakiness will always play out as anxiety, fear, or panic. Nothing will ever work. Nothing will ever be good enough for anyone.

I had locked the door to being loved, but nobody was strong enough to break through on their own. Nobody wanted it.

Jason had no idea what happened in that hotel room. That morning, the breaking news aired of Holbrook Elementary School in Connecticut: 27 kids slaughtered by a madman. The police were convinced that he was mentally ill, that he was antisocial, and indifferent to the feelings of others. I left CNN on and cried for hours. Crimes as horrifying as this shake us. Make us look for something to blame. Make us wonder whether mental illness alone could poison human characters to such an appalling state.

In the end, my mental issues tainted the trip entirely. I wrote the word "colorless" next to my details of the trip to Hawaii; Hawaii is anything but colorless. Not to mention we had stayed in a five-star hotel with a private beach and dined at Michelin-starred restaurants.

But there was no escape for me, no comfort.

"What's going on?" I asked him.
Jason looked up from his video games on Alienware to see a face filled with tears.
"The Holbrook news is so sad," I said.

He shrugged it off.

He later recalled his time in Hawaii as one of the most amazing trips of his life. Video games, new films, chatting with friends, and taking pictures. Jason was usually happy. He has always been amazingly capable of making his life interesting and comfortable.

But aren't we all responsible for our own happiness?

49. Neurologists

You cannot solve the problems with the same mind that created them. -
Albert Einstein

On top of the problems with my brain, my face decided to challenge me as well.

Over the years, the problems within my skull have increasingly caused the left part of my face to sag. No matter what facial creams I used, it has become asymmetric. No home remedies helped. Not soap, not makeup, not even Clarins facial lift.

This is proof that the body is intricately connected to the brain.

I started searching for help from a number of neurologists in Seattle, but none of them really took my problems seriously. As if they all had made a secret deal with each other, the answers were all one and the same. *Only a person that has been involved in a serious accident or is having a seizure would exhibit a serious imbalance in the face.*

But the differences between the two halves of my face were so obvious that even my friends at school noticed. "Why is the left part of your face swollen today?" my lab partner in physics class asked. I quickly made up stories of having allergies.

I turned to a shaman for help. Her name was Amy. After checking in with her spirit guides, she asked me to use my left thumb and pointer finger to press the meridian on top of my nose, just a little bit below the forehead. Within a minute of pressing this meridian point, a loud scary burp came out from some deep dark corner of my brain. It was the type of sound that would scare the hell out of anyone around me. After five minutes of pressing this meridian point, the left part of the face turned red, as if the brain had finally decided to bring some chi to the left part of my face again.

This meridian point, I learned later, was commonly practiced in modern acupuncture clinics to calm down the mind. Acupuncturists focus on this meridian for people who are anxious or have related symptoms. It indeed had opened some energies stuck within the brain. Later on, Amy taught me some tricks to balance the left and right sides of my face. When your left and right brain are perfectly balanced, the physical balance of the face results. One of the other tools Amy taught me was the method of alternative nostril breathing. She claimed that it was the quickest way to bring balance to the brain.

She was right. The effects were quite powerful, and the nose is exceptionally intelligent. In fact, alternate breathing is an ancient method that is widely used in yoga practices. A lot of yogis firmly believed that a lot of diseases are created by the problems of the nose. They believed that the left and right nostrils don't usually breathe in the equal amount of air during normal breathing.

This technique even boosted my GPA. Amy insisted that this method would calm my emotional state, in addition to helping restore the imbalances in the brain. She was right about that, too. I built a track record of good grades, proving that it is indeed a powerful way of bringing my mind to sanity—as long as I remembered to use it.

The pathetic amount of sleep I got before important exams made keeping my sanity even harder. A few rounds of alternate nostril breathing could quickly bring back the

balance. It instantly gave my body a much appreciated dose of calmness. *Everything is all right. I'm still breathing.* Usually practiced with my eyes closed, I started to access both sides of my brain during those exams. As a result, my words soaked the final essay in philosophy class like the rain soaked Seattle. In fact, the longer I invested in this method of breathing, the better the exam results usually were. It could be even more powerful than last-minute reviewing.

When doing alternate nostril breathing, this is what I do:

Step one: Use right thumb to close off right nostril.

Step two: Inhale slowly through left nostril.

Step three: Pause for a second.

Step four: Now close left nostril with ring finger and pause for 5 to 20 seconds.

Step five: Release thumb off right nostril.

Step six: Exhale through right nostril.

Step six: Now, inhale through right nostril.

Step seven: Pause.

Step eight: Use thumb to close right nostril.

Step nine: Pause for 5 seconds to 20 seconds.

When you can control your breath, you control your life too. And since a restless mind cannot relax, this little trick has been my savior on the road of recovery. No wonder many yoga practitioners incorporate this powerful method into their daily practices.

50. ※

Lives change like the weather

I hope you remember

Today is never too late to be brand new…

--"Innocent"

51. Alisa

Having given up hope of finding a traditional route to mental sanity, I continued my research into nontraditional avenues. I found help from a local shaman named Alisa.

She was one of the most renowned healers around the area. Many people claimed that she was nothing short of a miracle worker. Her willingness to share knowledge of endless possibilities had inspired many people worldwide. In short, there was every reason to think I was finally in good hands.

Shamanic healing is by no means the first choice in general psychiatry. As a matter of fact, many traditional psychologists label such alternative treatments "pseudoscience." What is science, anyway? To prove time and time again in the lab that this option does have positive effects? How do you demonstrate the different types of human experience in a lab?

Of course, a mainstream scientist could probably pinpoint an incident when an alternative therapy failed to improve a condition. The same can be done to mainstream medication. There is a lot of documented evidence showing that psychiatric hospital drugs can worsen the conditions of many patients, yet psychiatrists have no problems assigning them to new patients. To a person like me, shamanic healing was the only treatment that dramatically improved my condition. I had tried talk therapy too many times to know that the effects were minimal and temporary. My grandfather had tried to teach me Taichi, an ancient energy movement sequence from Asia which he could not live a day without. As eager as I was to learn, my mind was too chaotic to pay attention to the energy moving inside my body. A psychiatrist introduced by Kent School had once put me on Adderall to alleviate my ADD, and all it did was keep me awake all night.

Alisa's healing room gave me a warm fuzzy feeling like a mother hugging a child. It was located near Snoqualmie Park in Seattle. The room was decorated with pink rose quartz, flowers, and the most angelic music I have ever heard. Alisa struck me as a deeply compassionate person. She didn't circle around my mental issues. Instead, she went to the heart of my story. She taught me to focus on the present moment and gave me tools I could use to win the battle with the brain.

"Jiayi," she said, "have you meditated before?"

"I don't meditate," I replied. "My mind isn't focused enough."

"Are you sure?"

As far as I was concerned, meditation was only reserved for monks and nuns. "I'm positive," I said.

I never would learn how to become a energy healer. The only reason that I loved shamanic healing so much was the unbelievable clarity I have after each session. *So no meditation for me. No, Alisa, no. Just perform the magic and make all my problems disappear.*

Eyes are the windows of the soul. Alisa stared at me with her own stunning eyes, the deep laugh lines around the corner of her eyes. I could see that she knew what I was thinking.

"Jiayi," she said, "there are no magic pills for your problems to instantly disappear. Of course I can do my part and heal your energy system. But you have to perform your part as well. I have spent years of training for shamanic healing. I need you to learn skills to bring yourself back to balance when your brain is going into unwanted directions."

Her voice wasn't harsh by any means. She spoke to me like a seasoned master kindly admitting a new student. Alisa went straight to my weakest point of all—my utter lack of consistency. She later taught me numerous tricks, including heart mediation. She taught me to use the power of gratitude, one of the most powerful ways to bring good luck into your life. *What you give thanks to will be returned to you tenfold.* I began thanking everyone I encountered on a daily basis, and the effects were amazing. Within minutes after I thanked them in my heart, the person I thanked always brought me some type of benefit. It is indeed a remarkable way of turning your life around. She also taught me that it's important to be grounded and fully inhabit in your body. Alisa suggested that I walk on the grass in bare feet to connect to nature again. As bizarre as it sounded, I wholeheartedly trust her because of the benefits that followed all of her suggestions.

Of course, mental illness always comes with an expensive price tag. As unwilling as I was to delve into a spiritual path, I had no choice but to start learning meditation tools from Alisa. After all, many celebrities I admired, such as Kelly Rowland and Olivia Munn, all swore by the miraculous effects of meditation. Demi Lovato even described her meditation tools in her bestselling book *Staying Strong*, and credits them with bringing her to the enormous success that she has had today, as well as being her strongest ally in battling bipolar disorder.

As expected, Alisa performed magic on me. After half an hour of manipulation, she sat me up and described that there had been an energy block behind my left brain that was causing a lot of other energy blocks in my body. I could feel that she had removed something. She also explained that she had used Reiki healing techniques to realign all the chakras in my systems.

I thanked her and wondered how long the magical effects of this session would last. It turned out that I had no reason to worry, because I returned quickly. Every time I finished a session, it felt as if every cell in my body had been rejuvenated and I could face life with an unlimited amount of courage.

I might have been out of my mind, but I was smart enough to stick with my monthly shamanic healing session, the only thing that has helped in my world.

52. True friend.

"Listen," Audrey said, "I really need your help making this decision."

My best friend Audrey and I were in a Papa John's Pizza joint back in Shanghai. With us was Shirley, another friend. All of us were students in the U.S. now. We were just visiting China for the summer, almost like strangers in our own land.

They are the two friends I have had the longest. Both of them are super bright and are good with talking. But they were unprepared for what they found in the pizza joint. The new me was physically different: messy hair covering half of my face, a bit rounder face with wavering, unsteady eyes. I couldn't stop tearing apart the tissue paper in front of me.

"What's it about?" said Shirley.

"College. I don't know whether I should accept at Northwestern or Cornell."

Shirley started gushing congratulations. Then they both started gushing over how almost everyone in our former class at the foreign language school had been admitted into elite universities. Even our class monitor got accepted to Harvard.

I felt both happy for them and lost. Our school had been such a nurturing place that I started to regret ever leaving. What had been the point of going across the globe in an attempt to get into the best universities in the world? These friends from China could perform a zillion times better than my classmates at Kent.

Even worse, the new me felt somewhat retarded. I could hardly keep up with their lively discussion, even though it was in my native language. My brain had slowed down considerably. To distract me from the painful truth that I could no longer compete, I stuffed my mouth with one slice of pizza after another. Then I reached for more mozzarella sticks.

Shirley was watching me. "Jiayi, is something troubling you?"

Audrey looked concerned as well. I looked down at my lap. I wondered if they would laugh at me if I told them the truth, if they would abandon me.

Sobbing, I decided to tell them everything. How I could not make out half of what they had been saying, how my mental problems had become a hundred times worse at Kent.

"I'm sorry that I'm ruining the fun," I said, "but I just can't be myself." I started to tear apart another pile of tissue paper.

Audrey put her hands on mine until I stopped. "Dear, it's okay. We are here for you. If it's painful for you to talk, then just let us do all of the talking." And then she gave me a hug so tight that it could only come from someone who loved me immensely.

Shirley asked the waitress for paper and pen. They started brainstorming a long list of solutions of how they could make my problems go away. At the top of the list: *keep Jiayi busyregardless of the situation.*

True friends don't judge each other, and for the rest of the meal, they held my hands and eventually made me smile again. I realized something. There was no point in making yourself into a social butterfly, because usually there are only few people who will support and love you in any situation. In friendships, it's better to go narrower and deeper, rather than wider but shallower.

And Audrey ended up choosing to go to Northwestern.

53. ※

I'd like to be my old self again, but I'm still trying to find it.

-"All Too Well"

54. North Seattle

At North Seattle College, we were free to choose whatever courses we wanted in the first semester. The required courses were separated into two parts. One was for the high school completion program requirement, and the other was for the associate of business degree program. I chose to take philosophy, advanced calculus, and English 101 for the first semester.

The college campus was huge, yet everything was gray. Rumors had it that the North Seattle College was converted from a state prison. Till this day I still don't know the truth, but it sure felt like it at some points. Despite its stark appearance, the freedom that I experienced on campus was liberating. I no longer had to greet people and make eye contact with them. People came and went freely. A large proportion of the student population was studying part time, since they were much older and had already established their own social circles. Nobody really cared about who I was or where I had been.

That was just the way that I wanted it.

The introduction to philosophy by Dr. Olga Vishnyakova was mesmerizing. Dr. Olga reminded me of Mrs. Houston, the vibrant European history teacher in Kent. She came to the United States at a very young age, just before the collapse of the Soviet Union. Every class began with a seminar in the Socratic method of intensive questioning, which made us determine whether what we think we know is something we really know. She used to say that if we already knew everything, conversations would have been so boring.

Dr. Olga also told us that many popular social norms were based on mistakes in reasoning because those making them had never had the opportunity to study philosophy and logic. She made me start to question for the first time whether my mental problems and quiet nature had any value. Is it possible that introverts could bring smiles and beauty in this world as well? Is it possible that the battles with my brain might some day make me a stronger person?

Sitting in her classroom, I started to dream about becoming the girl I used to be. All shiny and new with a little girl's ponytail, the Jiayi whose almond-shaped face was lit up by a smile that melted everyone's heart. Thinking about that little girl, I sighed, feeling lost. I probably could never be her ever again. Nothing could really take me back to that state. Not knowledge. Not antidepressants. Not my new favorite philosophy professor Dr. Olga. Not reading the wisdom teachings of Socrates.

But maybe I could find a better self in the future.

55. Weight

A new ritual soon entered my life, and I know exactly why it started.

I began to weigh myself every night. Then, each morning, upon waking up, I weighed myself again.

I noticed something odd: My weight fluctuated a lot. Sometimes it was one or two pounds lighter than it had been when I'd gone to sleep. More usually, it was one or two pounds heavier.

When my weight went up, that number changed the tone of my entire day. It determined what kind of mood I would be in. It dictated my emotions. It reminded me of how powerless I was.

What sucked me into this new horrible obsession with weight loss was the inescapable fact that I had gained about twenty pounds during my year at Kent. The amazing variety of food in the dining hall was the culprit. As a result, I was no longer skinny. The moment that I began to care, the downward spiral began.

My mood affected my weight. On the days when I completely lost my grip on reality and failed to control my brain, I would end up gaining at least three pounds the next day, no matter what I ate. On the days that I kept myself on the winning side of my battle with my brain, I would win the weight battle too.

The morning following a binge day before I stepped on the scale generated the scariest feeling in the world. It felt like the morning after you remembered having drunken sex with a stranger. You knew you had done something wrong, but still magically hoped that your life would go on beautifully as though the episode hadn't happened. The scale never lies, even though I wish it could have been more lenient.

And therein, I got sucked into the spiral again. *No getting off this time.*

Soon I started hurting myself. I wanted to inflict as much pain on myself as possible. I fainted at the sight of blood, so I pinched myself as often as possible, as hurtful as possible. When I wanted myself to cry and I couldn't, I punched and slapped my head until I started crying like a newborn baby.

I became a tyrant, and my kingdom had a population of one.

Myself.

For a period of time, I didn't allow myself to swallow anything. *You don't deserve to eat. You piece of worthless trash.* The tyrant then took away the plate. All my food in the fridge was confiscated by the trashcan. Sometimes, the hungry peasant inside of me grabbed a plate of spaghetti my host mother had made for dinner and started shoveling it down my throat. But the throat refused to swallow anything. The tyrant then ordered my mouth to spit the food into the napkin. The action disgusted me. I was even more disgusted with the fact that I listened to his command.

Sometimes I chewed an entire bag of Oreo cookies, one by one, spitting each out. At this point, I wasn't sure whether the tyrant dwelling in me wanted to protect me from weight gain or turn me into a sicko.

I could hear the tyrant's voice: *Who are you to spit out so much food when there are millions of starving children? It's a sin. God doesn't allow that—wasting food and not caring about wasting. Who do you think you are?*

Then the peasant in me would respond: *I'm sorry. I'm so sorry. Someone ordered me to do it. I couldn't resist. I want to eat. I love spaghetti. I love food.*

Sometimes, after dinner, I grabbed another plate of chicken-fried rice that my host mother had made for me and went downstairs to my bedroom. I didn't want her to see I grabbed that much food. It wasn't normal. And I didn't need one more piece of judgment.

Not from her. Not from anyone

56 California Pizza Kitchen

Looking at the huge portion of salad I had finished eating in California Pizza Kitchen, I began to panic.

Oh my god, oh my god. Oh my god. Caesar dressing is more fattening than a hamburger.

I had read this piece of information on a health forum online. What had I done to myself?

On the other side of the table, Nancy, my classmate from calculus class, scrutinized me intensely. "What's wrong, Jiayi?"

Everything. Everything was wrong.

I had vowed to myself that I would only eat fruits and vegetables for a month and now the Caesar salad dressing had ruined everything. *The Caesar salad is as catastrophic to my mentalstability as the assassination of Archduke Francis Ferdinand was to Europe. One small act of violence is going to lead to all-out total war, and I don't have enough strength for this battle. I'm not prepared for another attack.*

Nancy could never understand. She drank Starbucks Frappucinos, which contained like 500 calories of empty sugar. She always got extra whipped cream too, every single time.

"Nothing," I lied. "You know what, I forgot my textbook. I have to go to my locker now."

Nancy looked at me suspiciously. "I would like to stay in the restaurant a bit longer."

"That's okay," I said, "but I have to go."

I left the money for the oversized Caesar salad and of its horrific dressing and walked out. I didn't care about Nancy anymore. All I cared about was protecting my mental sanity before the enemies break through. I should have known better.

Before I knew it, I had run to the gym at school. It was time for the treadmill. Run, run, run. Forget about everything. Forget about the Caesar salad dressing. Forget about counting how many people hated me today. Forget about the fact that I'm the most evil and imperfect creature on earth. Taylor Swift is my favorite, but I needed something stronger. I stuck my earbuds into my ears and blasted my head with Beyoncé.

I'm a survivor, I will not give up. I will work harder, I will survive and keep on surviving.

Ninety minutes later, I looked at the readout on the treadmill. 1200 calories burned. Thank God. I sighed again, feeling the endorphins running through my body. The fortress was still standing, the enemy had been repelled, the peasant was cheering. I was safe, for now.

But the war was far from over. There would never be total peace. A truce was not an option that my enemy had given me. It would keep fighting until I was worn down to nothing. How long would I be able hold on? How long would I last before deciding to throw my country all away?

57. Silver lining playbook.

"That was such a good movie," said my friend Emma.

We had just left an afternoon showing of *Silver Linings Playbook*. The only thing that Emma and I had in common was an obsession with Jennifer Lawrence.

"That part when Bradley Cooper went crazy in the house was funny but scary," she said. "I can't imagine living with someone like that." Her tone was condescending, but I held my tongue. "They're not as scary as you think."

"You never know," Emma continued. "They can't control what their brain does. One minute they smile at you. The next minute they could be dangerous to themselves and others."

I realized something. Emma was talking about mentally ill humans as if she were talking about another species. To her, mentally ill people were not human beings.

Most people with a mental illness are merely trying to live and thrive in their daily lives. They just have a wider spectrum of emotions than normal people. We are not that different. We are not another species. The statistics of sanity are that one out of every four Americans is suffering from some form of mental illness. Think of your three best friends. If they are okay, then it's you. - Rita Mae Brown.

The dividing line between sanity and mental illness is unclear. What if some people are naturally more emotional than others? They are labeled as having mood disorders. What about the people who prefer cleanliness? They are labeled as having obsessive-compulsive disorder. What if some people's attention spans are naturally shorter? They're labeled as attention deficit disorder.

Maybe it's going too far to say that there is no such thing as mental disorders. But I have met people who could be labeled as having severe depression in a mental health facility and who think they are perfectly healthy. Finding happiness is a natural process to them. And I've seen other friends who simply don't talk to people when they don't want to. They honor their feelings while other people don't. Once we are labeled as having a form of mental illness, we lose touch with our true feelings and live according to others' expectations. I am grateful for the sensitivity *Silver Linings Playbook* shows toward mental illness and wish that more media projects could be like that.

And I read somewhere that just as no one would ever go around believing they are 100 percent physically healthy, none of us are 100 percent mentally healthy either. We are all on a scale. To stigmatize mental health issues is to stigmatize every single one of us.

58 Pink diary excerpt

Hell must exist on earth.

I cannot persist one more minute. This brain condition is the worst hell any human being can go through. Hell is not some place that bad people go after they die. It's real. It's on earth now. Satan must have a hold on me and God must have chosen to ignore me. Or maybe I'm possessed by evil spirits. I probably need Pope Francis to perform an exorcism.

A million bits of self-pity ran rampant in my mind. Of course, I had forgotten that I had free will. I had forgotten that I had a choice not to victimize myself. I had forgotten that negative thinking does carry consequences. I had forgotten that every cloud has a silver lining.

Why can't I just stop fighting myself? Why can't I stop using the word I so much? Isn't it time to pay more attention to the outside world? Could my inner judge just accept the fact that there's no "should" or "should not"—only different approaches to the same goal?

59 whole foods market

A million needles began tickling my brain after seven hours of classes at North Seattle. I began thinking about the loud clock in the First United Church, the way it always screamed its familiar melody at 6pm. I loved that bell. The loud noise always seemed to quiet the chaos inside my brain.
Class ended. Another thought entered my head.
Whole Foods Market. I needed to get there. Knowing that food will never judge me, it was the only comforting place left.
When I walked inside, a black lady wearing an oversized apron smiled at me. "Do you want to try some samples?"oShe must have recognized me as I went there almost everyday for the sake of satisfying my taste buds as well as filling my pathetic amount of self-esteem.
"steem. have recogI took out the tortilla chips and scooped a huge amount of homemade avocado. The second I stuffed the satisfying combination of starch and fat into my mouth, something dwelling inside awakened.

"mething dwelling inside awakened. c need more."

The tortilla chips laying on the table all seemed too tempting. So I went for seconds, then moved on toward the shopping.

Organic apples, navel oranges, medjool dates, macadamia nuts—I searched every aisle for my favorite foods. After wandering around searching for more samples and weighing my groceries, I checked out.

" After wanddollars," the clerk announced. I did this almost every other day. Somehow Whole Foods Market has a magic charm of luring you back in to buy more even though you know that almost every item is overpriced.

The taste of the avocado sample started calling me again. Holding two heavy bags on each side, I went back in the store for more tortilla chips. And I couldn't resist filing more bags with yogurt pretzels, milk chocolate balls, and ginger snap cookies. Twelve additional dollars spent on junk food. Very nice. How my expense has skyrocketed after Seattle. All for food.

"Could I check your bags?" It was a security guard at least twice as tall as me. He must have spotted me eating more samples than my fair share and lingering in the store much longer than necessary.

Sure. I gave my bags and receipt to him. It's not like I'm hiding anything.

He checked every single item back and forth and try matching them with the receipt. Just when he thought I was as innocent as a blank white page, he pulled out a bulk of honey wheat pretzels.

"You didn't pay for this,"ou didn't pis voice carrying the feeling of victory. As if he finally caught a thief.

"What? I didn't?

My anxiety skyrocketed. How was that possible? Then I remembered tasting the samples of the pretzels. I must have forgotten to write down the code of the food while randomly throwing in the bag.

I immediately offered to pay. Instead, the guard took me directly to a manager's office. He asked for my identification, told me to sign something, and then banned me from Whole Foods for life. It all happened so fast that I didn't even have time to protest that I just bought over fifty dollars' worth of groceries, and that I was there every other day spending money on their overpriced goods.

But it didn't matter anymore. My last bit of joy from nourishment was taken away from me. I was immediately defeated. Walking back to the house, I took out my sunglasses and cried behind the shades.

The church bell announced the arrival of 6 p.m. But the chaos in my brain didn't stop this time. She started lecturing me that I was not only being banned from whole foods market for the rest of my life, but also by the entire world. Every bit of defeat felt like the end of the world.

60 . Pink diary excerpt

I spent a lot of time with myself in that basement in Seattle. Total isolation offered some degree of comfort and safety. As I watched myself sliding deeper into my head with no one watching or judging, I could barely wear the mask of sanity anymore. I didn't go upstairs to talk to Ben and Norma. They decided to leave me alone and I didn't care about them either.

Finally, Norma came downstairs to check on me. She saw me crying in agony while trying to figure out calculus homework.

"Jiayi, are you okay?"

Shocked to see her standing suddenly behind me, I struggled to compose myself. "Oh, I'm just homesick. Don't worry."

It wasn't a complete lie.

She grew compassionate. "You need to eat something. You didn't have any dinner tonight. You are getting too skinny.'

"Actually," I said, "I love eating. I have a lot of snacks in my room. I'm constantly eating down here."

I always hated when people judged my diet. At the same time, though, her concern felt good. It felt comforting and warm, as if she were taking care of something that's worthy of attention and love. As if I'm more than my weight. As if I could possibly be more than my shaky brain.

"Okay, dear. Let me know if you want to eat. I could cook more food for you."

She left the basement and went upstairs to watch television with Ben. I quickly went outside from the basement through my separate entrance. It was nearly dark, and I wandered around the neighborhood near the park, marveling at the beautiful scenery. Already February, it was still freezing cold here. I realized that I had escaped from the basement too quickly, without thinking, because I had only my shorts and shirt on.

I hadn't seen Alisa for four weeks. Maybe six, I couldn't recall. I had deliberately stalled the time between the shamanic healing sessions. The reason was that I wanted to see how long I could hold on to my sanity without others helping me.

I'm completely worthless. I'm a complete nightmare. Why would anyone have any compassion for someone like me?

I made my way back to the basement before the sky went completely dark. Nothing had changed. Nothing would ever change, not by myself.

I decided to see Alisa again.

61. Sleep!

The minute I met the shaman, I felt alive again. As if she carries the part of myself that I have lost along the way.

"How have you been?" she asked.

"I'm a disaster," I said. "My emotions go up and down. It's not that I care what my friends think of me. Mostly I just can't control myself. I can't make myself go to school or even sit for 50 minutes straight in one class. I don't think it's fair for other people to have to tolerate someone like me. I don't know the appropriate thing to do while interacting with others. I haven't even spoken with anyone in weeks."

Of all the low points in my life, this was the lowest. I was afraid to think that this was my destiny—to be petrified of small social interactions.

As the words tumbled out, I regretted my decision to spill my true thoughts to Alisa. She wouldn't understand. Mental illness is an isolating experience, and only people who have gone through it would understand. It might have been better to keep things superficial.

But Alisa didn't judge me. Her facial expression went from concern to deep thinking. I could tell that she was searching for tools in her practice that could help me. I grew optimistic that this down period could change, even though it had been longer than all the previous ones.

"How's your sleep?" she asked.

"Not so good."

"How much are you getting?"

"Maybe four hours a night."

Alisa made an *aaahhh* sound, as if she had found the answer. "Sleep is the foundation for optimum functionality for your body."

I later walked away from the session feeling confused. Was sleep that important? Was that the only advice that a shaman could give?

I started to force myself to sleep eight hours a night. If I had a morning class that required me to wake up at five o'clock am, I would put myself to bed as early as nine o'clock the day before.

That week was heavenly. I did not have one single food-binge. I didn't struggle with any weight issues. I had much less fear of others judging me. I was amazed.

62. Spring break: the spinning wheel

Spring break, and I was walking through a Shanghai fair with Audrey. We had both returned to our hometown for a week of relaxation. Audrey had just finished her freshman year at Northwestern University. She loved the place and had instantly made a lot of friends there. I didn't dare to tell her the truth of my situation in Seattle. I couldn't risk losing Audrey, too.

It didn't matter anyways, because I was happy at that moment. Everything seemed crystal clear, every sensation felt pristine. At that precious moment, I knew that I would trade anything I had to keep feeling this way. I was willing to bargain with God for anything. Money, beauty, luck—take all of them away. Just please let me keep feeling this way.

"Do you want to try the spinning wheel?" asked Audrey.

I looked at the wheel. It was a carnival game. Less than two degrees out of three hundred and sixty were devoted to the top prize. The rest of the circle was divided into smaller prizes such as stationery or books.

"Sure," I said, "why not?"

Audrey and I purchased tickets to spin the circle. We each had three shots.

The first time Audrey spun the wheel, she won a pen.

The first time I spun the wheel, the needle landed on the two percent of the circle. The impossible top prize. I couldn't believe my eyes. I was the first person in a month to actually win the top prize: a Swarovski crystal pen.

As the speaker announced loudly about the winner, some people started to gather. Some started to ask aloud how it was possible to win the top prize. After all, it's widely known that the needle is rigged to be impossible to win the top prize. After I happily claimed the blue velvet box, I took a deep breath and spun the wheel again.

A voice came into my mind. *It's okay to win again.*

I wondered where that voice came from. My higher self? God? A spirit?

Are you sure? I replied.

Yes, said the voice, *it's okay to win again.*

I looked at the wheel. It had landed again on the top prize.

The crowd shouted loudly. The manager came out of his office and stared at the wheel, disbelieving. He started explaining the precise reasons why there was no way the wheel could've landed on the top prize again. The chances were smaller than one in a million, he said. In fact, the company had only prepared two top prizes, and I had already claimed one.

"What's the other?" I said.

"A Swarovski necklace. But I don't think that this is legitimate."

Audrey pointed out that she had taken video of the whole process. After she showed it to the manager, he became silent. Then he gave me another luxurious blue velvet box. The Swarovski necklace.

A voice in the crowd said, "How is this even possible?"

I knew what happened. My mind had shaped reality. When I was in the best possible condition, everything was magical. The same had happened during my first week at Harvard. And during my childhood, too.

But everything comes with a price. I was capable of accessing a higher state of mind, but I was also capable of accessing the other end of the spectrum. The problem was that I wasn't in control. My brain made the executive decisions. The best I could do was to be brave in every situation.

Heaven or hell—it was all in the mind. If only someday I could make the decision of which it would be.

63. Easy breeze

For most of my high school years, I had woken up every morning with one thought in my mind.

How will I sabotage myself today?

It was hatred. I simply hated myself. But there was another person inside of me, one that wasn't yet formed, one who was trying to emerge a fully formed adult.

One day I started writing a love letter to myself. I just couldn't hold on to the self-loathing that I had carried for so long.

Dear Jiayi,

I know it hasn't been easy for the past few years. I know it's unfair to go through these troubles at such a young age. I know you have lost faith in yourself completely. I know you feel wounded and confused. But, my dear baby, could you protect yourself by loving yourself a bit more? Could you open up your heart to your own love and to others' love? You can't expect others to like you when you don't allow them to.

It's okay to get hurt. It's okay to fear. It's okay to run from yourself. It's perfectly fine to let it all go. Don't keep asking what should happen or what should not. Besides, who are you answering to? Your mom? Your family's expectations? This is your life and you should be its sole ruler. Don't hurt yourself, please, not anymore. Could you see how hurt your baby soul is? Could you allow her to breathe for a while? Could you put less energy into fearing and blaming yourself for that things will go wrong? And could you try to pay more attention to your overall wellbeing? Spread more joy and love?

Those are the most precious things in your life. And they are free.

I love you, Jiayi. No matter what happens in life, you will live. You are loved by the world. The people who love you will always love you. And I will always love you. I promise you.

Yours sincerely,

Jiayi

After writing down the kindest thoughts I had had in months, a dark cloud was lifted. I began to live with gratitude, the quickest way to any success.

It had immediate results. I thanked all my professors in my heart, and the more I used the energy of gratitude, the more I was able to learn from them. Although my mind still occasionally went to some strange place where I couldn't really think very clearly, I went through my last semester in Seattle like a breeze. I literally thanked my way to straight As. That's right—a 4.0. I visualized it, I made it happen.

It's all so easy—when you learn to say thank you.

64. Cairns

Cairns. Australia. It is one of the prettiest places on the planet. Spectacular corals, vibrant tropical atmosphere, seducing beach retreats. Everything you need to be happy.

Yet even in this paradise, my mind returned to its old habit. The brain decided to turn against me.

It's odd that this occurred there. It's not typical that my mind goes haywire during a trip. Traveling usually makes everybody, myself included, live in the present.

This was supposed to be a family-bonding trip. My mom flew in from Melbourne and my dad came all the way from Shanghai. The irony was that not only did we all rarely see each other due to our busy schedules, but also my dad felt uncomfortable being around mom without my presence.

See, last year was the coldest year of my family's Cold War. After my parents began to lead separate lives, their conflicts and arguments started to dissipate. Still, without me, a deadly silence filled the house. Our in-house maid, Chan, who had worked for my family for eight years, decided to quit, citing the excuse of having to take care of her children. Chan had always been a strong woman with clear opinions. I suspected that she was biting her tongue and refusing to take either side. Chan and I came up with some crazy plans to salvage my family, but nothing worked. After several failed attempts, she walked out of the toxic environment.

Of course, my parents were still putting up a front. To the outside world, we were a blessed and happy family. My father is a surgeon with a generous heart and enormous spirit. My mother is a savvy and inspiring businesswoman. Together they have a smart daughter who is studying across the globe in preparation for Harvard.

No one knew the truth.

I was nineteen years old, and my mental issues had consumed me for almost six years. I thought time was the magic wand that would heal everything. Yet the opposite seemed to be true. It was as if the more the body experienced a certain state, the more she began to adjust to that state. The body remembers being sad, confused, anxious, weird, or nervous. When a trigger arises, she decides to jump right back to that state.

The vacation felt as though I were walking on a trampoline. A sense of turbulence after unsteady movements filled in my space. I had trouble getting myself out of bed each day.

I dreaded each day. It meant at least ten more changes of scenery on the schedule. My brain ached in pain, but I didn't want to ruin the trip for everyone, so I went to all the previously scheduled attractions.

On the tour bus to a vineyard nearby, mom urged me to see the sheep, goats, and animals along the road. All I could do was to pretend that I was as excited as her. Meanwhile, my father tried acting smart. "Jiayi, did you know that there are eight times more sheep than the number of people in Australia?"

"Ha," I said. A dry laugh came out of my mouth.

I didn't care about his statistics. All I cared about was how my brain was suffocating me. I was seriously considering jumping out of the emergency exit window from the tour bus.

That voice of doubt began: *Hell exists, and it is this miserable body. My brain must be Satan. I have signed a lifelong contract to endure her, but now all I want to do is to rip the contract apart and start living somewhere else. I want to leave my body and go to the heavens.*

Then another voice corrected me: Don't be stupid. Your parents will be so sad without you here. They decided to remain friendly to each other just because of you. Maybe you really shouldn't be so selfish. I have to stay. How could I choose any other options when they have worked so hard to raise me?

I started taking deep long breaths and covered my heart using my hands. It seemed to work. When we finally arrive at the vineyard, I gathered myself together and my parents had no idea of the battle raging on the inside. We took the tour and learned about the vineyard equipment. Although the explanation from the tour guide didn't fully make sense, I wasn't annoyed. There were a few things I could still do. I could take pictures. I could laugh. I could joke with my parents. I could increase the value of each moment by thinking a little bit more positively.

I made a decision to breathe, drink some wine, and enjoy every miserable moment of the trip.

65. OCD period.

My OCD came along at the time when my brain started another weird jump. On a rare sunny afternoon in Seattle, I got stuck in my room. Every time I stepped outside, something in my mind forced me to step back. The OCD pattern quarantined me.

At the time, I knew my brain was steering me down a new slippery slope that I was not capable of dealing with. I started browsing the web, and a random YouTube video about faith and miracles popped up. A lady started talking about how we should trust the power of God more than the power of our problems. Just as I was about to close the video, a potential solution came up. *Maybe I don't have the power to stop OCD from happening all the time, but I can always choose how I will react. The tyrant in my head will always question whatever little things I do. But maybe this time, I could choose to trust God enough not to clean my desk for the millionth time.*

Miraculously, I was healed. I have neverexperienced another OCD episode from that time.

If only my other problems were as simple as that.

Two years after beginning my study in Seattle, I finally completed my associate of business degree. The whole adventure had taken much longer than I expected. I thought my AP scores earned in Kent would have shortened the normal two-year period of time, but they didn't.

Fortunately, I had enough luck to graduate and transfer to Johns Hopkins University. Not the Baltimore campus, though. I became an international business major at the Washington, D.C. campus. My AP scores, my academic work in Seattle, and my 2210 SAT score must've convinced the admission office to offer me a place.

In my heart, I knew none of this would have happened without Amy. I continued my sessions with her via Skype. She was the whole package: a gifted shaman, a distant energy healer, a counselor, and a therapist. Although sessions with her weren't cheap, every dollar was worth the price. But she made it very clear that she could not solve every single one of my problems. In *The Boston Globe*, Joseph Campbell, the late authority on world religions, once said the difference between a shaman and a priest is that "a shaman's authority comes out of his own personal and psychological experience. A priest is merely a 'functionary' to carry out rituals. When it comes to parenting and so many other situations, such as marital relationships, folks need shamans, not functionaries." That was true of Amy.

As I began my second year of working with her, I couldn't imagine a life without her healing gifts. The clarity that gradually filled my troubled brain after our sessions led to dramatic improvements in some areas of my life. I was able to normally talk to my friends again and even make new ones in Seattle. I've always used the ability to make new friends as a measurement of my worthiness. The countless methods Amy taught me about dealing with my mental craziness helped me on every single decision I made in regards to academic and social life.

Yet her work was only the facilitator for positive changes. I still needed to live my life, which meant that I had to make some decisions about my future career.

I had become increasingly drawn to the field of business. I was enraptured by the idea of opening my own company, since my condition didn't really allow me to work for anyone. I would never land a job in a prestigious firm like Deloitte. I would never work on Wall Street as I had once hoped. My best friend Audrey had recently been offered internships with both Morgan

Stanley and Goldman Sachs, and I was happy for her. Other than working periodically at a fish and chips shack, I had only ever been a student.

Still, I took comfort in the fact that my philosophy professor in Seattle had once told me that I was one of the smartest students she had ever seen. Her compliment had an enormous effect on me. I knew that if I could keep my brain's interest focused on one thing, I would be able to excel at it. How long could I keep that smart girl present? How much time did I have before she started to turn into someone else? I often begged her not to leave. *You are my true self. Without you, I don't know how to function anymore. Stay for a little bit longer.*

Sooner or later, that girl always left. Without even saying goodbye.

Another thing affecting my concentration was my diet. I often sat down with a large serving of fries and an entire fourteen-inch cheese pizza, wolfed the feast, then went to gym to run the calories away. After spending hours on the treadmill, I was too tired to think about my possible business ventures. Even my face became bloated after binging thousands of empty calories and carbohydrates. It settled the turbulence in my mind—but did so by bringing my mental processes to a complete halt.

I resolved to change all of this in the fall at Johns Hopkins. *I will be fine. I have to be fine.* As long as I continued biweekly sessions with Amy, it would all be good.

I hoped.

Time turns flames to embers

You'll have new Septembers

Every one of us has messed up too

--"Innocent"

67. Hopkins

Hopkins is not for the faint of the heart.

Thus warned Denise, the vice dean of Johns Hopkins University during orientation. The workload wasn't going to be easy.

The first day of orientation was a blast. Located next to the embassy of Australia, the Washington, D.C. campus isn't technically a campus, just a collection of few buildings. The dean of my program, Denise, gave me a huge hug. Her warm presence and the kind smile comforted my nerves. I was also making new friends in the transfer student group. Some had chosen to attend this satellite campus of Johns Hopkins despite offers from prestigious schools such as Columbia and Cornell. Some came with the enviable halo of being members of Mensa, a club only the most intelligent get to enter. Some, like me, came because the Hopkins international business program was the best offer on the table.

Once classes began, the amount of work I had to do was almost beyond my imagination. We were in class nearly eighteen hours a week, with an additional transfer student seminar each Friday. The business school's schedule consisted of classes no shorter than three hours. By the end of each one, my brain was screaming from the inactivity of my body and sent chaotic signals throughout my system.

The most daunting part of the daily schedule, however, was the socializing. The minute that I walked into the building, I felt obligated to greet my classmates. And that meant I had to be perfect every single day. I could not risk letting them know the truth, how I really felt on the inside. No one would be willing to know me after learning how chaotic my brain really was. I would become a pariah.

As a result, my anxiety skyrocketed the moment I walked onto the Johns Hopkins campus. As dramatic as it sounds, I nearly passed out once in an early morning accounting class. I hadn't eaten any breakfast, and I felt impaired.

As the weeks went on, I tried to ignore the gnawing suspicion that my new friends in the school secretly despised me. I tried to put aside the growing belief that my professors could see through my eyes and recognize the crazy turbulence occurring inside. I berated myself for not working harder. Some days I wondered whether my brain would explode right there in the classroom.

I guess you could say that my mind was like a brand new Mercedes. It cannot run forever without maintenance—fuel, water, etc. Some repairs along the way are minor, easy fixes, but some take longer. The maintenance team sometimes needs to keep the car longer so that they can be thoroughly fixed.

My brain was the car.

68. Ginny

The breaking point of any friendship in my life has always occurred at the moment that I feared the individual would judge my actions in any way. At that point, my behaviors would become forced and awkward. They weren't pretentious, just unnatural. The more I tried to make them natural, the more bizarre the behaviors would be.

I became friends with a girl named Ginny. We'd met during orientation, and she happened to be in many of the same classes with me. She struck me as one of the smartest girls I have ever seen in my life. She had a strong presence and aura. Although she looked tiny, her inner light was so powerful that everyone else in the classroom was affected by her in some way. And when she spoke in the classroom, it's as if all the air went straight in her direction. Even the professors paid close attention to her words.

As the days went by, I couldn't keep up with her brilliance. My brain started to become worse when she approached, as though it were admitting defeat. And every inch of my body felt compelled to get away from her. As she sensed my weirdness, Ginny started to judge me. She didn't actually have to say anything, though. The sharp look in her beautiful black eyes told everything. Her unspoken judgments came shooting at me like invisible arrows. And the more she acted that way, the more nervous I felt for being so imperfect around someone I admired.

When the brain won't stop shaking, it has to create stories. Profound suspicions of being disliked had been a huge part of my life for years. I couldn't begin to count how many amazing friends I had lost along the way, following the exact same routine. The fault was mine, though. How could I expect others to be comfortable around me when I couldn't be comfortable around them?

Later that semester, Ginny set her eyes on purchasing some land in the area of Virginia known as Tysons Corner. She tried to put together a team to do so, with herself as the sole developer. As she knew my father's real estate background, she started asking me about the land and the money she would need from me. She proposed that I invest $100,000, and she would personally spend five times more than that. I decided not to jump into the risk due to her lack of experience. Afterwards, she stopped talking to me.

I gave up trying to get her attention. In school, I didn't look at her at all.

Eventually she came to talk to me, during a class break.

"Hey," said Ginny, "are you upset today?"

"No," I replied, "just tired."

"Okay."

We sat in silence. Then Ginny continued. "I've been insensitive for the past few weeks. You're okay, right?"

No I'm not okay, I thought. *I'm not okay with you using me like this. I'm not okay with you silently pointing out all my flaws. And I'm definitely not okay with you thinking that I'm not worthy of your friendship.*

But what I said was, "Yes, I'm fine. You've just been busy."

She was still someone I admired tremendously. Her confidence, self-assurance, and intelligence were so inspiring to everyone who met her. After all, no one can harm you if you do not let them.

Cheesecake Factory.

My cravings for food increased infinitely the day that I walked onto the satellite campus of Johns Hopkins. It wasn't so much a need for food as a craving to fill the empty hole in my heart. It was a shouting and yearning for love. As if after stuffing something, anything, down my throat, I would be somehow worthy of more attention and affection.

My popularity at Johns Hopkins decreased within two weeks, yet I was able to make another good friend.

Sherry.

She was the only person that I could talk to comfortably without my brain betraying me. In fact, Sherry moved into my apartment in Crystal City not long after the beginning of the semester. I loved that she lived with me. I needed someone to keep me sane. She needed my company, too, as things had become more difficult with her boyfriend.

"How did your day go, Ji?" she said.

She called me Ji only when she was in a good mood. If her name could be shortened, I would have done the same. She spent most of her leisure time watching Korean dramas, cooking, and talking on the phone. It was the way of a lot of foreign students in the U.S. spend their time. Our homesickness weakens our drive.

Sherry's first year in DC had been tough. Constant arguments with her boyfriend and drama with classmates.

"It was okay," I said. "The class with John Kump was boring as usual. He talked about the story of his love for Italian food again."

"Italian food!" she said, her eyes lighting up. "Do you want to go out to eat?"

"Where?" I said.

"Cheesecake Factory."

The Cheesecake Factory near the Courthouse metro station was a dark, spacious place with a group of loving and warm staff. The delicious corn soup, the most amazing combination of shrimp, cheese and pasta, the warm smell of freshly baked whole grain bread always turn frowns into happy smiles. For me, whenever I went there, peaceful feelings arose, especially when I started to take a bite of the bread. For that moment, nothing mattered more than the pure enjoyment of eating.

Still, I was alarmed. I hadn't eaten any "bad" food (meaning carbohydrates) in a while. However, I could afford to be imperfect for a day. I still had the long weekend to lose weight after my binge.

We were seated and ordered quickly. I chose the jumbo shrimp pasta. Sherry continued to describe the latest volley of texts between her and her boyfriend. This time, he'd promised to take her to the Grand Canyon over spring break.

The food arrived. While she spoke, I noticed how she never seemed to care what she ate. It was surprising, since every girl is supposed to care how she looks. Then I noticed something else. My binge was going worse than usual.

First I finished my enormous plate of jumbo shrimp pasta, which weighed in at 2300 calories. Then I finished the basket of bread. Then I finished Sherry's strawberry cheesecake. Finally, I drank a large Pepsi.

I knew I'd done some damage. My bloated stomach proved it all. It was a grotesque feeling of knowing that you had fallen off the route to success. In one moment, I had decided that I was good enough to eat whatever things I desired. This particular binge felt different from normal eating, even different from previous binges. It was a feeling of losing control. It was a sensation of jumping on a mad horse that didn't respond to his master.

The binge got worse when I got home. I started ordering food on GrubHub, a popular app that enables people to get food delivered to their door at any time of the day. As the bright red words *It's time to eat!* jumped out on the screen, the last bit of my self-discipline shattered. I continued to order a double cheeseburger, a hot dog, and a cheese omelet. After it arrived, I scarfed the food in less than five minutes.

Then, at ten o'clock that night, I left my apartment and went to the closest 7-11 to get more food. I bought a box of dark chocolate covered almonds, a bag of Doritos, two cups of yogurt, a bag of yogurt pretzels, and an apple. As I walked past several drunk guys, a prayer came out of my insanely addictive mind: *God help me to be safe*. I continued eating food on the way. I forgot to take the fork so I used the cover on the top to scoop the yogurt and shoveled them down my throat.

By two o'clock that night, I had started to blame Sherry for my meltdown. After all, it was her casual, devil-may-care attitude toward food that led me to binge. I had a high school reunion the next month in New York City. How was that going to go?

With a mind as stressed and crazy as mine, something has to serve as a release valve. That something had become binge eating.

70. WBS

The morning after my binge session, I asked myself one question.

How do I rebuild my life from such a dark day?

I started thinking of what Professor Agresti in our project management course had taught us. He was one of the most compassionate and kindest professors I knew. He graduated from Harvard University and dedicated his life to teaching students. I instantly liked him during his first class and my brain agreed to stop battling me for a while whenever he spoke.

One of the things he taught us was the WBS, or work breakdown structure. I'm sure he didn't intend for me to use it to cope with my eating disorder, but I did so anyway.

1. Get back to 120 pounds.

   1.1 Fasting for 48 hours.

1.1.1 Starbucks green tea, 1st day.

2.   Coconut juice, 2nd day.

3.   Smoothies, 3rd day.

1.2 Only fruits allowed during school days.

1.3 New method: no eating after class (4:30pm).

1.4 New method: go straight to bookstore after class.

2. A better functioning brain.

1. No more TV watching.

2. Keep life interesting.

1. Writing down challenges.
2. Skype with old friends.
3. Call mom every day.

2.3 More regular sessions with Amy.

2.4 No more skipping lectures.

3. Get down to 100 pounds.

3.1 Intense high interval training, every night.

3.2. Eat no more than 500 calories for two days straight each week.

3.3 Pray for getting to 100 pounds.

4. Socialize more.
1. Attend more school activities.
2. Surround myself with the brightest people.

After I finished the list, I felt a bit calmer. Then I got on the scale and gasped. I had gained 10 pounds.

71

Try

Get your shopping on,

At the mall,

Max your credit cards

You don't have to choose,

Buy it all

So they like you. Do they like you?

Wait a second,

Why should you care, what they think of you

When you're all alone, by yourself

Do you like you? Do you like you?

--"Try", by Colbie Caillat

72. Arm Wrestling

It's like arm wrestling.

One force is sternly telling me to go out and fulfill my responsibilities, the other hand is screaming to let go of everything and stay at home.

It really doesn't matter which hand has stronger reasons. It just depends on who screams louder in my head. They wrestle, and one wins.

Some say that it's a challenge for people with brain abnormalities to even get up every morning. Sometimes that's true. I just take one step at a time. There's no need to jump ahead. I just hang in there and try to use all my force. Maybe this time, the hand with the right reasons can win. These dueling forces met on the battlefield of my soul, and their fights played out in a totally new way.

In my writing.

It all started the day that I was hiding in the garden cafe behind the business school.

The day had started out great. I had been in an amazing mood when I entered the classroom, but my brain refused to stay in that place. Everything collapsed. I had long forgotten how a normal brain felt. It hurt that I couldn't experience my true self. It hurt that my former self, an outgoing and bright girl, was nothing but a memory.

It hurt to feel amazed by the normal, functional human beings who surrounded me.

I ducked my head and ran into the bathroom. I locked myself in a stall, sat down, and started to cry.

Then I had a revelation. I decided to write down my feelings. No matter what words came out of my pen, no matter how ugly, they would help release this feeling of being unworthy and undeserving.

You are a piece of shit, I wrote. *You really are nothing. Do you think other people don't know what a weirdo you are? They all know. They just choose to not to disclose that to you. And they are much better than you. Even though you use strategies and tricks to get better grades than they do, they are still better. Their social skills, their positivity, their inner calm—you are nothing compared with them. Don't you know how imperfect you are? Don't you know that they are beloved, and that you are not? I hope you really know that, because someday everyone in the world will know it, too. They will tear you to pieces and Johns Hopkins will expel you and even your family won't love you. That's right, little girl, your day will come. And no Angels will save you then.*

My spirits actually began to lift after pouring those things onto the page. By this point, I was self-aware enough to know that this negative voice in my head was a monster that forbade me from telling the truth. He always ran so fast that my words started babbling.

I breathed out. Writing was therapeutic. It felt better than most therapy or medicine that I have taken. It was as though the sky started clearing up, and I was able to see the sun again.

I closed the notebook, stood up, and left the bathroom stall.

73 Ommmm.

Ommmmmmmm…

The sound of the heater in the school wasn't loud enough to battle the sound in my brain.

Ommmmmmmm. *Ommmmmmmmmmmmmmm.*

I started *omming,* too, because my brain couldn't stop shaking. Please God, make it stop. Make my heart open again.

It was the day after the bathroom stall episode. I hadn't improved, so I brought out my phone and called an expert neurologist in Virginia.

Her name was Veronica.

Upon walking into her office, she asked me to fill in various forms. Then she performed several tests on me. Those tests were so simple that as long as you weren't having a seizure, you could get straight As.

During the consultation, I started telling her every painful, numb feeling I had experienced on the left part of my face. I told her how my left breast was growing larger over time. I told her how the shakiness in my brain hurt so badly that it left me unable to concentrate.

She listened patiently, then said, "You are fine."

Before I could protest, she said that, from the perspective of her years of medical training as well as my new MRI, there was nothing wrong with me.

"No, I'm not fine," I replied. "I can't concentrate on studying at all. My facial expressions are so weird. My friends say that the left part of my face is increasingly lower than the right part."

I tried to remain calm.

"Maybe you should go see a psychologist. It could be all in your imagination. You could have depression."

I just stared at her. I couldn't believe a professional neurologist would offer such simplistic advice. Maybe the research on our brains is too minimal to understand anything beyond the usual strokes and seizures. When some experts didn't fully understand what they were seeing, they either tried to put labels on you or moved on to the next patient.

I walked out of the office, aware that life was, in fact, not fair.

After two days of denying myself food, the water and the tea in the apartment was simply no longer enough. I couldn't withstand the hunger one more second.

I left the apartment, blinking in the sunlight. It'd been two days since I'd stepped outside. I walked to the nearest CVS and bought a package of grapes and a can of coconut-toasted almonds. I'd always loved flavored almonds. I read the ingredients. It contained a thousand calories.

Ten minutes later, the can was empty.

The sleeping dragon within me was awakened. He led me into the Panera nearby and made me purchase a grilled fontina cheese sandwich and a macaroni and cheese entrée. I waited impatiently at the counter until the tasty food was delivered to my hands. I ran to a table and gulped it quickly. My stomach started to bloat, and I knew the impending judgment would come soon. So I ran back home and tried to get the subject of food outside of my brain for a little while.

There, my brain began to shake heavily. I began to cry involuntarily. The huge hole in my heart began to enlarge until it swallowed me from the inside out. *I'm not even the queen in my world, I'm just a slave, waiting to be beaten and whipped at anytime.* I couldn't even sit on the throne of an empire that had nothing but chaos and dust. What's the point of spending blood and tears to build a castle, knowing that it would eventually collapse again, as if it were made of sand?

Just forget it. It was never going to happen. I would never rule myself.

75 New Strategies

At the beginning of my second semester at Johns Hopkins, I started wearing glasses with colored lens.

I found those life-saving glasses in a tiny little shop near my grandma's old apartment in Shanghai. The artificial lights at the school had been hurting my eyes. Not only did these glasses mitigate my discomfort, they also made me calmer. They were not technically sunglasses, of course, because they allowed people to see my eyes, but they were enough to give my sensitive head some relief. They also took the focus off of my odd facial expressions and sagging face.

For the rest of my time at Johns Hopkins, I wore the colored lenses every day.

I also tried other things to change my situation. I began to say yes to everything—every single request from my friends, every single invitation to social events. I altered myself to whatever I thought they wanted me to be like. It took a tremendous amount of energy every day after school.

Facing my classmates became increasingly draining.

Still, I tried to develop other strategies to overcome social anxiety.

1. Ask questions during conversations.

2. Listen to others more. Because no one really cares too much about what you say during a conversation.

3. Act interested in other people.

I recited those strategies as if they were the Ten Commandments. As effective as they really were, eventually I knew I had to unhinge myself and let myself go and just be. It was too tiring, and although these techniques worked tremendously on some people, my appearance still made me one of the strangest people walking the campus.

I've learned not to waste my life trying to impress others.

I wiped the tears from my cheeks. A highly distinguished Johns Hopkins student, Li, had just committed suicide. I read his final post on social media.

After some period of sleeplessness and anxiety, my mind at least looks like my own again, you know, with some medication. Certainly, I am much less attentive to the outside world now.

Honestly I just wanna be a plain, normal guy, you know, but perhaps that's not the reality, right? The most I could do is just to have an everyday life, you see, going to classes, doing homework, getting around the campus. Finding joy everyday may not be as easy as it goes But for me I believe things are getting back where it should be, and that might be just what's needed.

The next day he killed himself. Nobody knows why. He'd even ended the message on a positive note.

I sat back, feeling that I knew what had happened. I couldn't remember how many times I wanted to kill myself. How many times I'd looked outside my apartment window and cried my eyeballs out. And how conveniently, just at the moment when I'd been crying hysterically and my nose had started to bleed, someone had texted me. My mother, a friend. This scenario had happened a lot. Those moments cannot be coincidence. It hadn't been my time to go yet.

But it'd been Li's time.

Did he finally decide life was no longer worth the fight? If so, I could relate. The feeling of watching yourself slip away is the worst. You remember exactly who you are, but you can't feel that person anymore. You wonder where that perfect child has gone. And there's not the slightest chance that the child is ever coming back. You ask yourself: what is the point of living inside this empty shell? Flesh and bones carry no meaning without the essence of the soul dwelling in it. The spark has been killed. Nothing matters anymore.

I wondered if things were different because he was a guy. My dad, for example, had always held my cousin to harsher standards than he did me. When I'd asked him why, he'd responded that if my cousin had been a girl, he would have babysat her like a princess. It's a harsh world for guys.

For the first time, I felt fortunate that I was not born male. I'm female. Even broken and unstable, I'm still a girl, and somehow the world is able to tolerate that. I don't have to be macho or strong all the time. I can show the world how vulnerable I am. There is strength in vulnerability. It takes a lot of courage to let another person inside.

77. Pink Diary Excerpt.

I looked at the trash bag in my hand and cursed myself. I had accidentally thrown the other bag that I had been carrying, a Barnes & Noble bag, into the trashcan of the 5th floor of my apartment building.

In that bag was my pink diary.

It was my life as it was my huge therapy outlet. I really couldn't believe how careless my brain was. I called the front desk and the maintenance guy came immediately. We pushed the giant green trash can out.

"Here's the gloves,ere's the glovesng them to me. I didn't even look at him. I didn't need the gloves. My brain was fixated on the pink diary. It meant everything to me—I doutlet for the turbulence in my mind and simultaneously a best friend. Just like Anne Frank's diary soothed her while being hidden behind her father thapartment, I was imprisoned in my head. And the pink diary had made the jail much more tolerable.

How could my mind carelessly drive me to keep the bag of leftover pizza boxes and throw away the diary? It was madness.

While the maintenance guy and I were ransacking the trashcan for the pink diary, people were throwing trash from upstairs into a trash can several feet away from us. We tossed aside perfectly wrapped Sephora bags and grocery bags while bottles shattered right next to us.

With each passing minute, my heart sank further. *Stupid brain. Freaky jumping brain*, a voice scolded me. I tried my best to ignore it and kept shoveling carefully.

I gave up eventually. There was nothing to be found inside. The maintenance guy looked sympathetically at me as I spotted the edge of the Barnes & Noble bag. I grabbed it and looked inside. It was empty.

"It's somewhere here!" I shouted. The maintenance guy sighed and kept searching the bin with me.

Eventually he stood up. "Look."

I lifted my head. In his hand was my pink diary, now torn and dirty.

I hugged the guy, clutched the book to my side, and felt reborn.

I needed to keep writing to live. It's like a life jacket to keep me afloat when the brain is dragging me down the water.

78. Life line

When you have a certain kind of mental disorder, you feel a lot like you're trapped on a sinking ship. Respect is like winning a seat on a life raft. Only after you board the life raft are you able to truly live. Only then will your problems start to fade away.

Ever since my brain decided to occupy more than its fair twenty percent share of oxygen, I felt inferior when meeting people who seemed much brighter and smarter than me. Whether it was their remarkable social skills, intelligence, or sheer beauty, my brain kicked my self-esteem until it was cowering in a gutter. I couldn't help but appreciate those amazing human beings who brighten up the world every single day with their brilliance.

Thomas West is the shining example of one of those amazing people. The oldest person in our class, at age 48, he was already a grandfather with adorable grandchildren. He was a retired warden who enrolled himself in Johns Hopkins to earn his undergraduate degree and keep fulfilling his desire for knowledge.

When I first appeared in school with those colored glasses, I asked his advice about whether it was appropriate. Thomas answered, "If that makes you comfortable, you should keep wearing them no matter what anyone else says. No matter what the rest of the school says."

Although he has lived a longer and much interesting life than the rest of us, he respects everyone's opinion. He's humble as well. While on the same presentation team with him, I saw that he tried to encourage everyone to speak as loudly as possible. "Forget about the professors and the grades," he urged us, "we are here to improve ourselves and have fun." His own public speaking abilities are excellent, yet he still wanted others to have the chance to speak.

May 20th was graduation day at Johns Hopkins, and Thomas West had 39 family and friends flying in to see him graduate. It was truly a testament to his character.

I wish that the world had more people like him. If everyone respected one another as equal human beings regardless of social status, family background, and personality difference. If everyone cared about each other a little bit more. When the neighbors in the building say hello with a smile, when you have a smiley face on your favorite Starbucks drink, when a stranger opens the door for you, your life suddenly gets a little bit brighter. All your problems seem so small and insignificant with the shining lights of human kindness coming in.

That's what Thomas West taught me.

79. Archangel Metatron

"Should I write about you in my book?" I asked the angel.

"Yes," the angel replied.

"But people won't believe it. They won't understand. They will point at my battles with my brain and accuse my imagination of being overly active."

The angel winked and smiled. "Just shut up and write."

His name is Archangel Metatron. He first appeared in my world when I was at Barnes & Noble, reading one of bestselling spiritual books by Doreen Virtue. She described the way that he has helped many children recover from conditions such as ADHD. Metatron uses a cube with sacred geometric shapes which in themselves are healing frequencies. Standing with the book, I mentally begged Metatron to help heal my brain using his cube. I didn't dare to speak it out loud. This seemed to be really off-the-charts weird.

Immediately after speaking that prayer in my mind, a loud burping noise came from the inside of my brain. Something started to open itself in my brain. A sense of clarity and a peaceful feeling came rushing through me.

He'd answered my prayers.

Every single morning since that day, I would call for his protection. On the days that I forgot to check in with him before leaving my apartment, I would have a less happy and less fulfilling day. The amount of stimulation on the streets of the nation's capital often set my brain on fire, but calling on Archangel Metatron to stand beside me keeps me grounded and immune to other people's bad energies.

I know this sounds weird, but I can feel Archangel Metatron when he arrives. He comes in the form of the vibration of the sacred geometric shapes, enters my brain with his healing frequencies, and brings me back to center. As one of the most powerful angels standing beside God, some say the highest of the archangels, Metatron is the go-to Angel to call for anyone who wants to connect with himself. He sometimes appears with white lights, which is maybe why he's also known as the Angel of Ascension.

He is also one of the only two Archangels, along with Archangel Sandalphon, to have been considered incarnated on earth. Archangel Metatron's close ties to writers, and his assistance with their delivery of the truth, also has been a huge inspiration for me. In fact, while I was meditating on the name of this book, he put a gigantic green mark next to the title *Battles With My Brain*.

Many people who are searching for spiritual development find Archangel Metatron to be the best possible ally in the quest for greater enlightenment and connection with God. Call on him when you are having a troubled mind and receive his help with an open heart. We all have free will that he can never interfere with. Archangel Metatron is always willing to help humanity. He's the most powerful friend you could have.

80. Envelop $$$

' Don't cheat on your envelope', instructed our professor. Make sure you label or mark every envelope."

Our favorite instructor, Professor Hemswridger was teaching us about budgeting and the importance of saving money. Each week, he asked us to put a certain amount of money into the envelopes, which were labeled *groceries, dining out, entertainment, clothing,* and *gasoline*. When the money ran dry from each envelope, the user wasn't allowed to spend more money until the start of the new week.

The lesson: you really don't have to save a lot of money to start benefiting from this system. It's really nothing new.

Another professor at Hopkins—Professor Mousavi—spoke of the importance of saving money as well. She explained the power of an interest rate. How saving three dollars each day amounts to 1095 dollars a year. Combine that with the right type of investment account, and you could become a millionaire in 35 years. Think of that when you go buy that cup of coffee at gallery cafe during the class break, she said.

My mom once said that people who treasure time and money are bound to be successful. I recalled all the money I spent at Whole Foods and decided it might be a good thing that I'ods andbanned from there forever.

81. Michael

Fears and phobia run rampant in my life when the brain cannot hold itself firmly. Typically, the thought of going to school each morning could send me into convulsions. My mouth would get dry and my face would go pale.

That's when I'd call upon angels to protect me. With their help, I felt much calmer in school.

One day, during a global economics class, the professor decided to randomly choose a person to go to the front of the classroom and deliver a twenty-minute overview of our recent case study.

"Jiayi," he said, "come on up."

As the panic ran through my spine and directly to my brain, I felt like I was going to throw up in front of the whole class. Then I called upon Archangel Michael, the leader of all the angels.

At that moment, I was so vulnerable that I heard him clearly. A sudden surge of courage came rushing in my body. He reassured me that it would all be fine. He made me realize that this could be a good opportunity to overcome my fear of public speaking.

I resolved to face the daunting situation with courage, and slowly drew to my feet. As the professor asked me in front of the entire class to illustrate some advantages and disadvantages of globalization, I immediately cited the example of how the people of Melbourne have kept the global company Starbucks out of their market. Melbourne is famous for its coffee culture and strives to maintain its coffee culture intact from the process of globalization.

The professor seemed to be loving the example. Then he kept pushing other questions. How do we view the process of globalization? How do we take advantage of it?

"Globalization has brought many benefits into my life," I explained. "As a constant traveller, seeing my familiar stores around the places I visit brings joy and stability to my life. And I guess that's why some global companies are widely successful."

I scrambled for something else to say. *Throw the question back to him*, said the archangel.

"Professor," I said, "how do you personally enjoy the trend of globalization?"

The professor began telling personal stories of his executive friends at Pepsi. Then he sent me back to my seat. I felt relieved.

Ever since then, I have always called on Archangel Michael before giving a presentation. His response is instantaneous, and he helps with any situation. While Archangel Metatron is the most gifted healer of the brain, Archangel Michael chased away fear and instills courage. And amidst all the uncertainties of my daily life, my angels' constant reassurance and help are the only things that I'm sure will never fade away.

82 Greece

"A large-scale exhibition in Greece is asking for a Chinese-English translator," said Emmy, a coordinator at Johns Hopkins. "Are you by any means interested?"

"Me?" I said.

"Yes, you."

"Of course," I replied.

"That's great!" Emmy replied. "It's a two-week-long exhibition with several renowned artists flying from Asia to Greece. Your main responsibility will involve a lot of translating, as well as helping with the registration process for events."

The more I thought about it, the more it sounded like something that would require highly skilled socialization. And I'm the furthest from that.

I decided to go anyways. The opportunity to visit Greece was simply too good to pass up. It's one of those places that will always attract millions of tourists from around the world regardless of the direction of its economical change. It's a place that tourists seem to never forget.

"Email me all the details of the event," I told her. I was a bit startled at my rare decisiveness. It sometimes takes me hours to even decide whether to go to school on a certain day.

The event was to be hosted during the two weeks before Christmas. The team consisted of thirty-nine highly renowned Asian artists who would be exhibiting their artwork in various museums around the country. We would be traveling to Athens and Corfu together.

The day after I finished my final exam in international marketing, I boarded the flight.. Completely worn out, I slept all the way from Washington to Geneva, where I connected on a different flight to Athens.

Fifteen hours later, I stepped onto Greek soil. The first thing that came to my attention was the different atmosphere of the country. It felt like an agricultural society rather than a highly developed one. In many ways, it had stayed closer to nature than other seemingly sophisticated nations. Its simplicity and beauty were refreshing.

And there were animals. Dogs and cats ran wild everywhere on the streets. Walking from the

McDonalds located in the center of Athens to the nearby hotel, I petted and fed three large dogs. Along the walk, plenty of chapels and churches showcased the deeply religious roots of this nation.

But I wasn't there to play, or sightsee, or worship. I was there to work. The first three days in Athens were marked by much laughter and bonding with those well-known artists. They seem so normal yet so special. Most of them were quite humble and friendly, although a small percentage of the team seemed to be signaling that they were too cool to hang out with an inexperienced student like me. But I decided to focus on the positives.

The journey affected me in a very important way. Dressed in professional attire and high heels every single day, I gradually developed a more professional attitude. Something switched in my brain once I was dressed up in professional attire. It was as if my inner businesswoman had been awakened. Regardless of my state of mind, work was work. I learned to put other people's important business before my brain's monkey business. The steadier I appeared to be, the more trustworthy and reliable I appeared to be.

For a time, I felt like I had overcome my problems. I had stopped thinking so much about myself.

83. Achilleion Palace

What I remember most from my trip to Greece was the Achilleion Palace on the Corfu islands, but not for the reason that most tourists remember it.

It was where I saw the angel.

It was named after Achilles, a Greek hero of the Trojan wars, and the favorite character of Empress Sissi from Homer's book the Iliad. Although Achilleion begun as a summer palace for the Empress Sisi of Austria, it became her permanent home after her son died.

My mother decided to visit me at the end of the trip. That morning I prayed to God and the angels that would enable me to have an amazing day. I prayed that the Archangels Michael and Gabriel would surround us all day and bring us peace and joy.

As we arrived at the Achilleion, we discovered that we were the only two tourists in the entire palace. It was the winter season, and Corfu didn't have that many tourists. The amazing palace with its wonderful statues, exquisite gardens, and breathtaking views was waiting just for us.

Soothing classical music was playing in the background. My mother and I became fascinated by the palace. We felt the presence of Empress Sisi.

On our way to the third floor of Empress Sisi's bedrooms, my mother told me that she felt that something special was about to happen. We were taking pictures of one another when suddenly I gasped. A gigantic angelic figure appeared in the large mirror in the hallway, just in front of the upstairs bedroom. He was pristine white and carried a large sword.

My mother had almost reached the third floor. I immediately dragged her up the few remaining steps, and she caught a glimpse of this beautiful creature before he vanished from the mirror. In my mind, I knew it was the Archangel Michael. I had prayed to him earlier that morning. I didn't really believe that he would take my prayers seriously and offer us protection.

When we went to the top floor and opened the notebook for tourists to write on, we found that there was only a small blank space left on the last page of the book, as if it had been reserved for us. We drew a huge heart in the space and, alongside it, wrote about our amazing experience. We felt deeply humbled by the opportunity to visit the beautiful Empress's favorite palace.

As we both processed the angel encounter, I understood that I would be all right no matter what I would go through. The angels would always be with me.

84. IB interview

If I am done being a victim, it's only because I have learned how to become a liar.

The most important day of my life—an interview for an internship at the most challenging investment banking company in China—and my brain is threatening to sabotage everything.

It was my summer break in Shanghai. After knocking on the door of the company and giving the front desk my résumé, I had been surprised to receive a call from the human resources department three days later. *This must be a joke*, I'd thought. The company is famous for rejecting ninety-nine percent of their internship applicants for no apparent reason. It has offices in New York, London, Shanghai, and five additional places.

They wanted an interview.

I eagerly agreed. Later that week, I arrived at the office in my best professional attire. They seated me in a room and told me to wait. My hands started to sweat. My brain began vibrating.

Then a staff member signaled that the CEO of the company was about to come to the office, and it almost went haywire. I forced it back into line.

The CEO entered. "Hello, Jiayi," he said.

Good. The CEO seemed so nice. It was a good start.

A team dressed in professional attire entered behind him. They examined me from head to toe. One of them finally asked, "Tell us why you want to join our company?"

I delivered the sentences exactly as I had rehearsed them. "This corporation is a global brand that carries prestigious value. Working here would be an excellent opportunity to learn about the culture of investment banking, where I will apply the knowledge I have learned in college."

I delivered it with poise. *Score*. I congratulated myself silently.

"Could you brief us about the knowledge and skills you have learned at Johns Hopkins that could be useful to our company?"asked the CEO.

There was a long silence after this question. The CEO moved his eyes from his notes to my eyes. A woman started clicking her pen. Another coughed.

"I have learned many things at my university. Besides all the financial models that were taught in our finance classes, I also have developed very good communication and social skills." That, of course, was a total lie.

After more questioning, things began to go smoothly and they seemed quite satisfied with my answers.

The woman who was clicking her pen asked me the question I had been dreading. "Is there any challenge that you have that would potentially deter your excellent performance during this internship?"

God, there were *so many* things. They grew like a poisonous mushroom against the inside of my skull. I would be randomly late for no reason other than my weak determination to start another day. I would be a happy and carefree person and a moody ass the next day. My weight would balloon for no discernible reason.

"No," I lied.

They were done questioning me. The CEO gave me a handshake and led his team outside the conference room. I almost collapsed after the door had closed.

They gave me the internship. My brain was still as potentially disastrous as a sleeping volcano, but I had prevailed.

I had lied. Both to them, and to myself.

85. Internship.

Despite those initial lies, I started to feel quite comfortable with some of my new colleagues in at the capital investment banking firm.

As busy as the internship schedule was, the work was quite easy to handle. I had two supervisors, a tall senior manager with a cold manner, and a former Morgan Stanley VP financial analyst with the exact opposite demeanor. And when they asked me out one-on-one or in small groups for coffee or lunch, I managed the opportunities quite well. Every meal felt like an opportunity to make new friends. I even pushed myself to ask my supervisors or my colleagues out to lunch. After all, as weird as I possibly seemed to be, it was only a two-months internship.

My colored glasses became a huge issue, however. A VP asked me in the printing room what the hell I was doing wearing those glasses in the office. I replied that I had a medical condition and that artificial lights made my eyes uncomfortable. She didn't believe me and didn't say another extra word. I wasn't entirely lying. But hiding a truth felt like a lie. The glasses were good at masking the sagging left side of my face. They were also there to mask the constant changing of my facial expressions. How could I explain those things to her?

During a lunch at K-11, the most stylish mall in Shanghai, a group of financial consultants joined our four-person circle. I started to panic, as I'd acquainted myself very well with the people close to me in the office, but these were new.

Sensing my fears, a manager named Jeanne who was sitting nearby began talking to me. She had recently converted to Buddhism. Not so long after getting to know her, I shared with her how I believed that Kuan Yin had guided me closely along the way. Jeanne immediately showed me the Kuan Yin pendulums that she had been wearing since she was a little kid. She converted to

Buddhism recently but had always recited Kuan Yin's songs religiously every day. We became friends after discovering that we shared these beliefs. I didn't tell her about the Angels. People seem to only believe one thing at a time.

After that, Jeanne started helping me in various ways. She definitely sensed something was wrong with me, but her kind actions made me believe that it's possible to be loved, even in a business setting. She took me under her wing, as if someone had finally decided to toss a piece of bread to a starving puppy.

As the first few weeks went by, I surprised myself by thinking of opening my own business. I hadn't thought about entrepreneurship. Jeanne told me numerous stories of how twenty-somethings had already started their own businesses and become widely successful. One of her clients, in fact, was only six years older than me and was already seeking millions of dollars of capital investment for her clothing line for pregnant women. Another of her clients owned a store via Alibaba and had earned huge profits as well.

I thought about all of this, unable to decide what area of business I wanted to venture in. Is there any market need that hasn't been fulfilled? Could I be of any use?

86. Grandma

A great aspect of interning in Shanghai was the amount of quality time I got to spend with my family. I hadn't spent any serious time with them for years, not since I had left for the U.S.

I especially missed my paternal grandmother, who had raised me since infancy. Because she' recently had leg surgery, she asked me to move in with her during the internship. Her amazing decorating skills had always amazed me. For my bedroom in her house, she rearranged the furniture, added flowers, and papered the walls with beautiful blue-colored star wallpaper.

With a living environment like that, everything became easier, and I felt myself gradually starting to heal. Every morning before I went to the internship, my grandma would make me a power protein smoothie. It consisted of a type of five-bean soymilk (blackberries, kidney beans, soy beans, chickpeas and green beans), whole natural almonds, one cup of walnuts, and Lingzhi powder (a traditional Asian superfood). Usually one cup of this powerful concoction was enough to sustain me the whole morning, along with the apples, peaches, and kiwis that she insisted I carry with me to work.

During the time I lived with grandma, I started to realize that what you put in your body does have a huge influence on how you feel and what you look like. I ate super clean and mostly organic fruits and vegetables. My acne cleared up within two months. My brain issues have started to heal themselves.

You are what you eat. It simply cannot be disputed.

87. Kuan Yin pendant.

The Kuan Yin pendant on my neck suddenly became larger. The Mother Mary of the East enlarged before me, along with her lotus and her dragon. She's glowing in white light. I wonder what my grandma, a firm believer of Kuan Yin, will think of this beautiful sight. She always says that her amazing daughters have been given to her by Kuan Yin. The goddess leaned over from her dragon and said, "Call on the dragon, for he represents my strength." *Then she raised her voice.* "I will fix this."

I woke up from this bizarre but beautiful dream, wondering whether it was just another creation of my overly active brain. I had started to wear the Kuan Yin pendant because my grandma had insisted that the pendant she got from the Buddhist temple would bring good luck.

In fact, I had become Christian for a little while after going to boarding school. Singing in the choir and learning Bible stories from theology class made me a believer. When I had asked my grandma to join the Christian group, she'd insisted that she could not because Kuan Yin has watched over and blessed her throughout her life. I'd asked my theology teacher about Kuan Yin, and he'd replied that she embodies true compassion and love.

Now, three weeks later, I accompanied my aunt on a four-day trip to Da Nang, Vietnam. It's a gorgeous place, and on the second day of the itinerary, the tourist guide brought us to an island. Upon landing on its shores, I couldn't believe what I saw.

An enormous Kuan Yin statue.

It was taller than any of the other buildings in the city. It was pristine, white, and peaceful. The tour guide explained that she's the tallest Kuan Yin statue in Asia. Ever since she was built, the typhoons that had affected Da Nang for centuries stopped occurring. And the tour guide also explained that no other building surrounding this island is allowed to be taller than the statue.

I immediately started crying. My dream had been real. I did have a chance to be all right again. Kuan Yin was accompanying me along the journey, along with Archangels Michael, Metatron, and Gabriel.

They will fix me. I have no doubt about that.

88. U.S. Chamber of Commerce.

I spun around, realizing that I couldn't find the representative from the embassy of Finland.

It was the SAIS Global Conference on Women in the Boardroom, sponsored by Johns Hopkins and hosted at the U.S. Chamber of Commerce. A panicked feeling rushed through my spine. Emmy, the Johns Hopkins coordinator, so brilliant in organizing the important parts of the event, had left me in charge of room two for the discussion meeting after the plenary session.

The ambassador was supposed to be in room two. Yet she's nowhere to be found. The session started without her, but I didn't know whether I should rush outside to find the ambassador or sit there taking notes as Emmy instructed.

This time I was dead for real.

Mrs. James, the managing director at a high profile business development who sat on the boards of major companies such as Time Warner, started addressing the matter using her powerful voice. "arner, started addressing the matter using her powerful voice. elopment t there

Then I saw Susan. The lead coordinator from Hopkins was looking in the door to see what was going on in the discussion room. As the only official person in the room, I tried my best to write down every single thought produced by those incredibly powerful women.

"—our stats show that northern European countries—"

The speech forced me to think about the matter of the ambassador again. I ran out and told her about the situation.

"Oh, Jiayi, don't worry.' Susan told me that the representative has gone to group three for the discussion period." She thanked me for being so detail-oriented while she should probably thanked my brain for exaggerating the seriousness of the situation.

I rushed back inside the room trying not to interrupt any important discussions by those influential people.

As the discussion went on, I marveled at their utter brilliance. I kept wondering, if my brain settled down, would I become someone like them in twenty years? Someone like Mrs. Johnson, a serial entrepreneur who had already established five successful global companies and kept on being at the forefront of innovative entrepreneurship? Or the HSBC Vice President, a short but brilliant woman whose opinions were so penetrating and strong? Or the president of KPMG who was so kind and considerate, even when I bothered her for some basic information about their company's internship program?

The EU ambassador even came during the keynote speech.

After the meeting, I rushed to Mrs. Johnson for some entrepreneurial advice. I thought that she would probably just write me off and walk away.

However, upon hearing my entrepreneur ideas, she seemed so fervent and agreed to sit with me, postponing her arrival for the reception hosted at the embassy of Australia. When I told her of my dreams of developing a brand, she told me the most important thing is to label the brand in a grand marketing way so that no other brands could outdo it. She then shared her personal success stories with me. Her willingness to talk with me, a nobody, was a huge confidence boost. She continued to say that she would love to mentor me as she could see something in me. It was then I suddenly made a decision to work towards my dreams despite my long history of problems. If a successful multimillionaire business founder could see anything in this girl, then there might be some potential in her. And all I had to do was to take a leap of faith.

89. Venture.

A friend in Shanghai whose baby is two years old asked me to purchase powdered milk from the U.S. When I asked why not just buy milk powder through vendors, she answered that she doesn't trust them anymore. There had been too many news stories exposing the dangers that Chinese milk powder can potentially cause in babies' health.

This gave me an idea. I returned to Shanghai with 30 kg of powdered milk from Karicare and gave it to her. More importantly, I registered for a food permit and to begin the Jiayi International Company. Obtaining this food permit took some time and effort. I also registered the company, which embodies all types of industries.

The goal was to literally sell all kinds of things. We are allowed to import and export food and other goods. With us serving as a medium, many Chinese people will no longer need to worry about food safety. Though the material will be mostly imported, we began looking to launch our own product lines to save on costs, including powdered milk. We are a team that has a vision in our mind that can literally change the food problem in china.

While developing my company, I had to be able to converse about topics such as golf and European travel with other entrepreneurs at association meetings. A few even had interests in crystals. Some of them really liked to share their own personal stories. They would begin with "Back when I first started... " And instead of yawning, I would tell myself to remember everything I heard. I became an avid learner of others' experiences. Because I was so young, one way I could be successful in business was through learning from others.

Their stories inspired me in so many ways. Since then, they have been invincible rocks, there to support me when I felt down, when I wondered whether it was worth it to get unbelievably low grades through online courses to achieve some seemingly impossible dreams.

90. Hopkins Graduation.

The year that I finally graduated from Johns Hopkins, Pixar President Edwin Catmull delivered the much-hyped address at Homewood Field.

It was a freezing, rainy day. Thousands of students and family members huddled beneath raincoats and umbrellas.

"In truth, all of our movies suck at first," Catmull said. "I don't mean this in the sense that I'm being self-effacing or modest, I mean this in the sense that they suck.y But that's part of the creative process, he continued. "I believe that everyone has the potential to be creative. It is our choices that block or enable potential in others and in yourself. Make it okay to make mistakes.o

I listened to him, utterly rapt. I didn't even feel the cold. This was the person responsible for the record-shattering *Toy Story* movies.

"How do you become more creative?' he asked. "Creativity is the process by which we solve problems, whether they're a story, on the job, a relationship with partners, or societal problems."

I listened as he continued to address the importance of embracing failures. He told us that failures actually fueled the creativity of his team. Thinking of my budding trading company, I realized that my success might happen more quickly if my brain did not force me into isolation. Changes do not come into your life until there's a shift from within.

He finished his speech to dampened applause. Even though the graduation gown could barely shield me from the coldness of the pouring rain, my spirits were soaring high. I had graduated from one of the best universities in the U.S., even with the cold howling wind against me. I had just been inspired by an amazing businessperson.

The brain could not tear me down, not if I kept my spirits intact.

91. Tai Chi & Chi Gong

Sitting on a train with my grandfather, I read a frantic text from Sherry, my roommate at Johns Hopkins.

There's no such address as Licheng Donng Rd

I told her I would visit her hometown in Jinan to seek out a Chi Gong group. Ioupread on their website that Chi Gong could heal the spine and brain naturally. My grandpa, who had been practicing Tai Chi, had decided to go along with me. As the train passed out of Beijing, I was being told that the address didn't even exist.

Then Sherry's mom called me.

"Jiayi, please don't go. Sherry asked everyone in the family and no one knows such a place even exists. We have been living in the area for all our lives and if the Chi Gong retreat really is as beneficial as you say, the people would have already come."

My grandpa heard what she said and insisted that we take the next train back to Shanghai. However, I was determined to try to find the Chi Gong place. I jumped into the taxi upon arrival at Jinan and told the driver of the address.

"Oh, Licheng Dong Rd. It's so far away and is in the rural area. What are you going there for?"

' visiting a relative,' I lied.

Grandpa cut in. 'We are going to a chi gong retreat."

"A what?" The driver stopped the car.

"Chi gong. We saw on website. Have you heard of it?"

"No, not really. I have been a taxi driver for over ten years and no one has asked me to go to that place. It's a very rural area and is hard to get to."

I insisted the driver continue, even though my grandpa pleaded to go back.

Then the Chi Gong master texted me to arrive by bus, not by taxi. As much as a bulldog as I was, the tone of the message made me ask the taxi driver to turn around just when the car approached the mountains and when my grandpa's face became paler.

On our way back to the train station, the taxi driver kept saying how sketchy and dangerous those places are. There are many disgusting stories of how groups of people would kidnap hotel guests, rip out their organs, and sell them. The driver said a recent tragedy occurred when a young girl got drugged in a hotel and a gangster group sold her kidneys for millions of dollars.

I truly felt sick now. I couldn't believe how far I would go to try to heal myself. I probably could never forgive myself if anything would happen to my grandfather.

We booked the next train back to Shanghai. Grandpa looked relieved. And my heart felt as heavy as stone.

92. Teacher Ma

On the train back, my grandpa kept talking about how we almost got killed because of my stubbornness. That's all I could think of too. His words were exactly like what my brain was saying.

"Why don't you start learning Tai Chi with me?" he said on the train back.

I never believed in Tai Chi methods, although it have helped my grandpa throughout the years. Grandpa claimed that he never could live a day without practicing his Tai Chi ten sequence combined with some Chi Gong methods. He also said that on days that he didn't practice Tai Chi, he felt much less energetic. Considering he's 80 years old and still sharp enough to be the accountant of my mom's trading company while moving around like a teenager, I agreed with him and started practicing.

During my summer break, I encountered Teacher Ma, a renowned Tai Chi practitioner with thirty years of experience. As she scanned through my body, she felt that there was a blockage at the back of the brain that needed to be cleared out. *Gosh how uncomfortable it must be to live with a brain like that*, she said.

She asked me to sit down in the park and gather the chi in my brain to clear the stagnant energy. After several rounds of trying, I felt much lighter emotionally. Most importantly, I felt calmer, as if a bird who's trying to break through the window finally realized that that it wasn't the right way to go through, although it seems to be clear and transparent.

Teacher Ma had many students globally. One time she asked if I could do her a favor by translating for a woman from Colorado who was coming to visit. The woman was so happy to see Teacher Ma that she broke into tears. She was in a late stage of cancer and the doctor said it was hopeless. She could expect to die in two months. After the session with Teacher Ma, she said that she wished she could do what Teacher Ma has done to her body. I saw the utter bliss and joy on her face that I haven't seen on any walking human being's face for a long time. Two years later now, she's still living healthily and happily.

Afterwards, Teacher Ma told me how Chi changes lives for the better. One of her students, Bianca Molle, was healed from Parkinson's disease in 13 months and even published a book on the experience. Teacher Ma herself has gone through severe disorders and counted Tai Chi as the biggest blessing of her life.

She taught me to view my brain problem as a blessing. *Jiayi, when you truly become healed,* Teacher Ma said, *you will be an expert at healing others as well.* And she kept on saying that when you find methods that work for you, it becomes an obligation to use your experience to help as many people as possible.

93 A start-up.

In life, true success is never handed to you. You have to continue to earn it, a lesson that my parents set for me. All of a sudden, interning at the most prestigious investment banking company in Shanghai wasn't good enough anymore. I needed to start something unique.

I needed to start a business venture.

As I learned from a marketing professor in Hopkins, the best kind of business is about fulfilling a market or solving certain problems, while making profits at the same time. I had an idea about designing and selling unique souvenirs in Greece. I felt incredibly anxious the moment that I emailed this business proposition, my first one, to a Greek friend. In my mind, the idea was quite workable. In reality, it was nothing particularly new or creative.

Regardless, I went to register my own international trading corporation during lunch break. It was literally the hottest day of the year in Shanghai. The metro ride from the finance district to the registration center seemed to take forever. My youth and inexperience aroused quite some attention at the registration center. *You are not even twenty?* said an officer. She examined me with suspicious eyes, as if I were in no way qualified to open my own company. As if I should be prepared to look for my parents.

Paperwork after more paperwork. Question after question. Interrogations after interrogations.

Background checks, requests for new documents. The process was overwhelming. I breathed deeply and vowed to do whatever it took to go through the process. It was just beginning, and already I was intimidated.

Finally, after a week of traveling back and forth from the office to the registration center, my own international trading corporation was finally registered and approved. It was ready to fly.

Greece might be having economic downturns or financial problems, but the tourists' market will always be booming. My friend in Greece had urged me to contact factories in China to design new products. The stars started to align. I searched on the Internet and found a factory that manufactured souvenirs like necklaces and sculptures in Jingdezhen, a city famous worldwide for manufacturing porcelain and china. It's the origin of the Qingtong culture in Asia. I contacted the company, and after countless hour of negotiating, the factory finally agreed upon a price and design pattern that I presented to them.

The first shipment arrived at the port of Athens two months later, shortly after the end of my internship. I started to feel the pressure of being the only investor. I had plunged what little amount of money I had made during the internship, and every single dollar that was left in my U.S. bank account, into this venture. That bank account had been set up to pay my tuition and food at Johns Hopkins. What if this didn't work out? What if all those products went to waste? What if no one bought them?

Some of the pressure was real, some imagined. But it made it all the more terrifying. I'm sure, when people know that these products carefully polished with pictures of Greece sceneries were designed and produced by a 19-year-old, they would be wondering what the hell she had been doing. I was worried that I would be exposed as a girl who only lived in her brain and could never go anywhere with her troubled head.

But thanks to my Greek friend, and his wide social network, the first shipment of souvenirs were sold out with 27 days. His contacts had made all the difference in distributing and selling the products. And by the time I returned to Johns Hopkins for my last semester, my corporation had already hired fifteen employees.

I came to realize that actions mean everything. My actions had lifted me out of the paralyzed state in which fear had quarantined me. Merely surviving in the world is never enough. Surviving and thriving could be hard for normal people, and a hundred times harder for a person battling with a damaged brain. But I could still succeed if I kept myself busy.

The key is to forgive and to focus on the positive aspects of life. Otherwise, you poison yourself while hoping that your problems will die. After all, I eventually realized that everyone carries some kind of baggage. Some people are just better at hiding it.

If you keep searching for the light, there's no doubt that you will find a way through the darkness.

94. MRI.

The sixty-year-old doctor gasped. He was staring at the MRI of my spine.

I held my breath. It was hard to imagine what could make a seasoned doctor like him gasp. After conducting 24 hours of an EEG, MRI, and CAT scan on my brain, the number six hospital in Shanghai insisted that nothing was wrong. A nurse joked that I should probably check myself into the psychiatric department.

As a last resort, my dad urged me to do a MRI on my spine.

"It's an inverted and completely twisted spine. Normal people have natural curves with their spine. A straight spine will cause some people to experience headaches and even mental issues. But yours is inverted and twisted. How's that possible? You are only 19."

He pulled a picture from a file.

"Look at this. This is the spine of a 70 year old who went through the MRI machine before you. Even his spine is much healthier than yours. At least he still has the curve."

He recommended me to start physical therapy immediately. He then taught me many methods of taking care of the spine. *Stop looking down at your iPhone now. It will take a long time to recover. It's sometimes not even possible for the bones to grow back. Wait, have you had an accident?*

Walking outside the hospital I felt relieved after finding some answers for my brain issues. For several years, I did everything I could to check on the brain. Yet every time nothing came up, except one time a young doctor claimed that there wasn't enough blood flow coming to my brain.

Who knew the spine could be the culprit? Now I remember laughing off Audrey's remarks during a sleepover on how unsupportive and soft my bed was towards the development of the spine. It all made much more sense.

95. All is well?

I would be lying if I said that everything is okay today.

I just had a huge binge session yesterday. Half a pack of Pop Tarts, three sweet potatoes, two apples, a huge bag of pretzels and two Snickers bars. With such a huge amount of food in my stomach again, I found myself wondering if I've truly healed. Apparently I haven't.

But the difference is this: I *feel* better.

What has made me feel so improved? One is the change of my attitude. I no longer care too much. I won't cry over things like overeating anymore. Everyone indulges once in a while. I remember being a young girl gorging myself on cake, potatoes, sweets, and chocolate bars during Christmas. There was not an ounce of guilt in me, and I was always the perfect weight. I also remember that there were days back then when I didn't feel like talking to anyone, but I didn't label myself as antisocial or depressed. What triggered all the problems at the very start was the shift of the focus from positivity to negativity. From seeing the good to only seeing the bad. The truth is that what you focus on expands in importance. That's the ultimate law.

Perspective is everything. I find myself laughing at my problems and mistakes nowadays, as if those imperfections aren't mine. When I sense judgment from other people, I just brush it off my shoulders. Most are imaginary, anyways.

I also try to feel the energy of pure joy. It's still hard to feel peaceful or calm, since my brain does act up from time to time. However, joy is an emotion that's easily accessible as long as I have enough gratitude in my heart. There are so many people and spirits to be grateful for. My mom and dad, my family, my friends across the globe, my archangels, Kuan Yin. All give my life meaning.

You can never separate the body from the mind. While we can eat the most nutritious food, the mind also shapes the body. I'm always at my thinnest when I think I'm good enough. Being surrounded by people who love me during the summer vacation back home, I lost almost 15 pounds in a month. Yet when I went back to Hopkins during the last semester, I ended up gaining all the weight back. Depression, bipolar disorder, or any mental issues affect our entire body, our beauty, and our skin.

In fact, there was a famous experiment that clearly shows us how self-esteem influences our view on how others see ourselves. The New York Times explained it.

Dr. Robert Cleck, a psychologist at Dartmouth College, has devised an experiment that illustrates how body image affects how people think. Using theatrical makeup, researchers fashioned a scar on female subjects before their interaction with a stranger hired for the experiment. Unbeknown to the women, the scar was removed before the face-to-face conversation with the stranger. Nevertheless, the women said the stranger had stared at the scar and made them uncomfortable.

In most cases, others view us the way we view ourselves. A good friend of mine from Seattle, Nancy, once asked me why I was so defensive the first time we met at the school. I told her that I thought she hated me.

"You were looking at me with a weird facial expression," I said. "You obviously didn't like me."

"Are you kidding me?" she replied. "I was observing you because I thought you were a cool girl! Why do you think that?"

Then I realized something. The critic wasn't them. It had been me all along.

96. Strategies.

Whenever I feel myself spiraling down into self-doubt, I have several techniques for rebalancing myself. Here are a few.

Classical music

Listening to classical music is one of the quickest ways to rejuvenate your energy. My favorite piece for bringing clarity to my mind is *Etude No. 1 in A-flat major, Opus 25*. Its fast-paced melody generates fresh air around me and brings me back to center. Whenever I can, I open up my iPhone and start playing classical music, this piece in particular.

Chanting the sound *om* and *gong*

Om is the sound of the universe. When you speak the word, the primal energy of your essence starts to channel through your body. When I speak this word, I literally feel all my chakras start to open up. And my brain starts to work much better. When I'm taking an exam or feel unsteady, I just chant *om* quietly and let it work its magic. Your world is a reflection of your inner state, and this sound restores your inner universe and brings peace to your system

Unlike *om*, which connects you to the energy of all that there is, chanting the sound *gong* clears away all the imbalances in your body. One time when I was on a boat to the Great Barrier Reef, I suddenly felt sick. The fruit and milk I had for breakfast started surging to my throat. I quickly started chanting the sound *Gonggggggg. Gongggggg. Gonggggggg*. Within seconds of repeating that sound, I felt completely fine, as if nothing had happened. A lot of people on the boat that day got seasick, but I wasn't one of them.

Shamanic healing sessions

These were the main transformation, particularly my sessions with Alisa, Amy and Susan. When countless talk therapy sessions, professional psychiatric counseling, neurologist counseling and even Freudian psychoanalysis failed, they were the only people that could help on a deeper level. I'm not saying that those other traditional methods don't work. It's just that shamanic healing sessions played a much more important part in my healing journey.

Watch ELLEN

Watching Ellen DeGeneres on her talk show ELLEN has brought so much joy into my life. When I get depressed from time to time, I open ELLEN's YouTube channel and literally laugh for hours. Joy is an emotion of high frequency and it uplifts everything by changing your perspective on life.

Daily prayer and writing

I keep a prayer sheet stuck to my bedroom wall and recite it every single morning. Writing down my feelings is also hugely helpful. There's something magical about putting down exactly what I feel. It focuses my intentions for the day.

Smile

A smile is as brain-stimulating as 2000 chocolate bars.

-Research from study.

By the simple act of smiling, we become happier. We appear more positive and attractive. I often think of my best friend Audrey, who is a bundle of joy and always smiles as often as possible.

Joy is an emotion of high frequency. When we experience positive emotions like that, everything in our life shifts. We look at things from a different perspective. And a positive attitude leads to a chain reaction.

Pursue dreams

"I think of work 24 hours a day. Because nothing else is worth my brain activity."

- Fan Bin Bin, Asian actress.

Dreams keeps us alive. Pursuing them keeps our attention away from our problems. I once feared getting frustrated by my inability to concentrate. Then I realized that there are many ways to achieve something.

High intensity interval training

This is a form of exercise that involves regular bursts of high intensity workout with short periods of rest. It leads to better results in terms of fat loss and cardiovascular benefits. Our brains often work the same way. By dividing tasks into several small tasks that can be achieved within 20 minutes (instead of the equivalent of jogging five miles straight), we might find them easier to achieve than we thought.

The 45-second plank

A magical movement. Virtually every exercise has the potential to give you a mood boost. Plank is the ultimate king for the brain. It relaxes muscles groups that become stiff and tense after long hours of sitting. And when the length of this simple movement reaches 45 seconds, your brain will benefit from extra blood flow, and that will start to balance your entire system. It's my secret stress reliever while tackling challenges.

Alternate nostril breathing

It's the simplest and most effective strategy of all. The brain needs enough oxygen to function. When your mind is dull, concentration and clarity are poor. Alternate nostril breathing brings equal amounts of oxygen to both sides of the brain for improved brain function. Five minutes of this before an exam or interview is a great way to access your whole brain for improved performance.

Nutrition

Let food be thy medicine and medicine be thy food
-Hippocrates

This subject alone deserves a book, and many have been written—The Paleo Diet, the Beauty Detox Solution, and many others are all great introductions to how our bodies process food. Personally, learning about nutrition has saved my life. I don't believe in diets anymore, which only brought me more binge sessions. My mind functions much more clearly when my body is clean.

On a day when I blend all the nutrition into smoothies or eat mainly fruits that are mostly water, the day will go magically well as there are no *clogs* in the body.

My morning brainpower smoothie is the secret weapon in this tiring battle with the brain. My entire body feels nourished after drinking this brainpower smoothie and my brain functions as if she is normal again. Here is the recipe:

Brain Power Smoothie

2 tablespoons of chia seeds (ultimate brain food)

1 scoop of soy/brown rice/hemp/egg white protein powder

1 tablespoon of flaxseeds

1 tablespoon of hemp seeds

13 raw whole almonds

1 scoop of super collagen (optional)

1 tablespoon of raw cacao powder

A tablespoon of spiralina (another superfood that has powerful effects on the brain, but too much has the potential to ruin the entire smoothie)

2 pieces of calcium tablets (optional)

Blend all of them in a Vitamix or a similar blender. There's nothing to be afraid of with a breakfast like that.

Listen to your body. Keep the strategies that make you feel good.

Eat less, occasionally

It takes a lot of your energy to digest food. It's better to limit your intake, and choose brain-nourishing food. Ingredients that are close to nature and high in protein are most ideal for the brain.

For instance, on my first day traveling in Greece, I indulged in the most delicious five-star hotel breakfast buffet anyone could ask for. Freshly-squeezed orange juice, Greek yogurt with walnuts, chocolates, raisins and honey, traditional Greek milk pie, extra-syrupy Greek samali pie, almond cookies, chocolate soufflés, scrambled eggs that melt in your mouth before you start to chew, mixed beans, mashed potatoes, Greek-style pancakes layered with chopped walnuts and syrup, and dozens of other unbelievably delicious items.

For the first hour afterwards, things seemed fine. However, for the next six hours, my brain became like a jungle. Monkeys jumped out of nowhere and a thousand species of birds flew without their usual elegant order. Things around me became bizarre. When the ambassador asked me to translate her words to a local artist in the Byzantine museum in Corfu, I could barely come up with easy English words to describe what I was hearing. When a group of professional artists tried to use me as their model to take good photographs, I tripped on the stones in the old fortress on the island. Thank God I was several steps away from the edge, or else I could have fallen right into the sea.

The following morning, I faced the same amazing buffet breakfast. Instead, I filled my plates with assorted fruits, a bit of yogurt, and fresh orange juice. The second day went absolutely magical.

Your true home is your body. Treat it with respect and gratitude. Love it and honor it.

Einstein's view of prayer

It was 1936.

Einstein, already a Nobel Prize-winning scientist, had just escaped the Nazi regime and settled in the US.

A young girl named Phyllis wrote to him asking a question that was puzzling her Sunday school class.

The question was essentially this: "Do scientists pray?"

Her letter and Einstein's reply is copied below for you.

The Riverside Church

January 19, 1936

My dear Dr. Einstein,

We have brought up the question: Do scientists pray? in our Sunday school class. It began by asking whether we could believe in both science and religion. We are writing to scientists and other important men, to try and have our own question answered.

We will feel greatly honored if you will answer our question: Do scientists pray, and what do they pray for?

We are in the sixth grade, Miss Ellis's class.

Respectfully yours,

Phyllis

January 24, 1936

Dear Phyllis,

I will attempt to reply to your question as simply as I can. Here is my answer:

Scientists believe that every occurrence, including the affairs of human beings, is due to the laws of nature. Therefore a scientist cannot be inclined to believe that the course of events can be influenced by prayer, that is, by a supernaturally manifested wish.

However, we must concede that our actual knowledge of these forces is imperfect, so that in the end the belief in the existence of a final, ultimate spirit rests on a kind of faith. Such belief remains widespread even with the current achievements in science.

But also, everyone who is seriously involved in the pursuit of science becomes convinced that some spirit is manifest in the laws of the universe, one that is vastly superior to that of man. In this way the pursuit of science leads to a religious feeling of a special sort, which is surely quite different from the religiosity of someone more naive.

With cordial greetings,

Yours

A. Einstein

Facts about mental illness

Gender differences occur particularly in the rates of common mental disorders: depression, anxiety, and somatic complaints.

These disorders, which predominate in women, affect approximately 1 in 3 people in the community and constitute a serious public health problem.

Unipolar depression, predicted to be the second leading cause of global disability burden by 2020, is twice as common in women.

Depression is not only the most common women's mental health problem, but may be more persistent in women than men.

Reducing the overrepresentation of women who are depressed would contribute significantly to lessening the global burden of disability caused by psychological disorders.

The lifetime prevalence rate for alcohol dependence, another common disorder, is more than twice as high in men than women.

Men are also more than three times more likely to be diagnosed with antisocial personality disorder than women.

According to a study, women are more prone to the internal disease side of a mental disorder while men are much more likely to suffer from an external disease such as substance abuse or antisocial behaviors. In simple language, women keep things in and men lash out when it comes to mental illness.

Positive affirmations

I am more than a body. I am body, mind and soul. I am worthy of love.

I am worthy of my own self-love and self-acceptance

My body is a sacred temple and I treat it with respect, kindness, appreciation, and love. My life matters.

I'm capable of doing anything I put efforts towards. I am not a burden if I ask for help from others.

I am more than a number on my scale.

I love myself even when I am unhappy or depressed.

I allow myself to feel whatever emotions I have. I am on my way to recovery.

I am surrounded by positive and loving people.

My life is full of blessings regardless of what I have gone through.

I focus on positivity in life as I know that my thoughts create reality. I am deeply loved by God and angels. I'm supported by the universe. I am a unique and valuable individual.

I can succeed in this world.

I am learning more and more every single day. I forgive myself. I love myself.

I deserve respect and set boundaries with rude and judgmental people.

I express my needs and feelings clearly and communicate them in a respectful manner.

I am empowered by my journey through obstacles. What doesn't kill me makes me stronger.

I do not give power to the SHOULD monster. There are many routes to success and many ways to do one thing.

I am sober, happy, and full of life.

I embrace every opportunity that comes along.

I stare down at the emotion of fear and write down my challenges.

I accept the fact that my mental problems or anxiety will happen, but I don't give them more power by fearing them. I focus on what's truly important and use strategies to move past them.

I make the best of every situation.

I'm fully present at this moment. After all, it's all that matters.

I accept all of what I am.

It's easy for me to express my feelings and needs if I don't judge them. I treat myself like a loving parent.

I allow myself to live fully.

I am not alone in this human experience. Even if I am, at least I've got a story no one has told.

I take full responsibility for who I am and what I do.

I love my parents for they have given me life and done so much for me. I am a survivor and I will keep living. As long as I live, there's hope.

I am more than my past experiences.

I love life and I love God.

References:

Tolle, E. (1999). The power of now: A guide to spiritual enlightenment. Novato, Calif.: New World Library.

"Here's What Einstein Told A Sixth-Grader About Prayer." The Huffington Post. Web. 13 June 2015.
"Key to Happiness: Simple Act Makes You Happier than 2,000 Bars of Chocolate Can." DeseretNews.com. 30 Sept. 2013. Web. 13 June 2015.

"NAMI: National Alliance on Mental Illness | Mental Health ..." Web. 13 June 2015.

"Mental Health Myths and Facts | MentalHealth.gov." Web. 13 June 2015.

"Quote of the Day: Broken Hearts." EllenTV. Web. 13 June 2015.

Virtue, Doreen. The Angel Therapy Handbook. Carlsbad, Calif.: Hay House, 2011. Print.

Blakeslee, Sandra. "How You See Yourself: Potential for Big Problems." The New York Times. The New York Times, 6 Feb. 1991. Web. 13 June 2015.

"Pixar President, Co-founder Ed Catmull to Speak at Johns Hopkins Commencement." The Hub. 30 Mar.

2015. Web. 13 June 2015.

Songs:
Beyoncé, Kanye West, and Jay-Z. Beyonce I Am -- World Tour. Music World Music / Columbia, 2010. CD.

Swift, Taylor, Dan Wilson, Max Martin, Shellback, Jacknife Lee, Gary Lightbody, and Ed Sheeran. Red. N.d. CD.

Swift, Taylor. Speak Now. Big Machine Records, 2010. CD.

Caillat, Colbie, Babyface, and Johan Carlsson. Gypsy Heart. Republic Records, 2014. CD.

Young The Giant. Roadrunner Records, 2010. CD.

Swift, Taylor, and Nathan Chapman. Fearless. Big Machine Records, 2008. CD.

About the author: Jiayi H.

Jiayi is the founder of Dragon Pacific International Corporation. She recently graduated from Johns Hopkins

University with Bachelor of Science. She's a lifelong learner, traveler, writer and animal lover.

www.ingramcontent.com/pod-product-compliance
Lightning Source LLC
Chambersburg PA
CBHW031347040426
42444CB00005B/214